A History Louisiana: 1858 to 2013

Scott Crawford

A History of Soccer in Louisiana from 1858 to 2013

First edition: 2013

LAprepSoccer Publishing Co.

© Scott Crawford 2013

CONTENTS

Foreword	6-10
Timeline of Soccer in Louisiana	11-22
1858-1895: Immigrant Football	23-46
1895-1904: Association Football and Athletic Clubs	47-61
1905-1907: The Rebirth of the New Orleans Association Football League	62-77
1907-1908: The Amateur and Professional Split	78-91
1909-1918: American Football's Triumph Over Soccer	92-95
1912-1922: Dock Soccer Origins	96-101
1923-1925: Central American Soccer Arrives in Louisiana	102-112
1926-1949: German and Latino Soccer Rules the State	113-129
1950-1958: Clubs and College Converge in League Play	130-139
1959-1969: Carlos Ross Mitchell, ISLANO, and the New Orleans Timbers?	140-156
1967-1983: Immigrant High School and Youth Soccer	157-171
1984: Jesuit's Win Over Warren Easton: The Big Picture	172-179
1985-2013: The All American Sport	180-191
Conclusion	192-195
Appendices	
Boys High School State Championship Games	197-202
Head Coach Records in Boys H.S. Championship Games	203-204
Girls High School State Championship Games	205-209
Head Coach Records in Girls H.S. Championship Games	210-211
All State MVPs, Gatorade POYs, LAprep XI MVPs	212-214
St. Paul's Holiday Invitational Results	215
Notable Louisiana Referees and Assessors	216

What is history but God revealing himself?

Herbert Butterfield

To be able to fill leisure intelligently is the last product of civilization.

Arnold Toynbee

Foreword

In 1985, my parents introduced me to soccer at Lafreniere Park. As a child, I did not think about what the game was, who had played it before me, or any of the questions about the game I later asked. It was simple – I liked playing. Playing soccer remained an integral part of my life throughout my youth and into my college years. Soccer was how I met many of my friends and introduced me to the idea of teamwork; it was my instrument of exercise; the game taught me how to win, and more often, how to lose; soccer gave me an escape when I needed one. Soccer has given me many good things over the years.

As with anything we appreciate and care for, I wanted to know more about soccer. The problem with that desire was that in the 1990s, there was not available much public information about soccer. In 1999, I was in college and my brother was still playing soccer in high school. I was starved for knowledge about the game, so one evening on a whim, I started a website that would become LAprepSoccer.net. The website is predominantly devoted to the high school game, which I believe is the key to making soccer an integral part of American culture. At first, I only hoped to compile scores from around the state and create accurate rankings from those scores. That idea sorely underestimated the number of others who also wanted knowledge about the youth game in Louisiana.

As LAprepSoccer grew, I dove deeper and deeper into the papers to find out how this sport developed. Until this past year, I thought Louisiana soccer started in the early decades of the twentieth century and faded away, only to resurface in the 1960s. Even then, there is much history to remember. When I discovered that soccer traces its origins in this state back to the 1850s, I was shocked, and quite honestly, thrilled.

All this time, I thought I had been among some of the earliest players of the game in Louisiana. When I realized soccer predated me by more than a century, and that all of this history had been forgotten, I decided I would make the bold and possibly preposterous attempt to write a shorty history on the sport in the Pelican State.

The vast majority of the research that went into this book comes from primary sources, namely newspapers. While it seems to be a growing trend in many fields to read what others have recently written about a subject, there is no historical substitute for contemporary accounts of any subject. For that reason, and others, members of the press have a holy responsibility to report accurately and honestly. Newspapers, likewise, have a heavy burden to focus on truth rather than become tabloids, especially in this age of internet and celebrity. A word of encouragement to members of the local press who cover soccer: your words matter. They are read today, and they will be read in the future, perhaps even 500 years from now. Make what you write count.

Some readers may be disappointed when they see how little writing is devoted to more recent soccer, namely the 1980s to 2013. This was no accident. More happens with soccer in Louisiana during this period than any other. However, history requires perspective, in my opinion. I, therefore, did not feel comfortable writing extensively on this recent material.

While the research for this book was nearly fifteen years in the making, the writing has a less industrious past. Two weeks ago, I realized I might never again have two solid weeks to write. So I began writing. Two weeks later, this is the finished (or not-so-finished) product.

This history will surely be flawed. It will exclude many important figures and events in the game's development; it will wander from themes that may be poorly explained and connected; it will lack many of the elements a good history requires. I hope those whom I inadvertently exclude will forgive me. The flaws of this history, however, are not reason enough to prevent its writing. The history of soccer in Louisiana has for too long been neglected. I hope people will use this history to learn, but more than that, to write their own histories of the sport so that we can better understand how soccer formed in order to better know where it might go.

So many people deserve thanks for contributing to the creation of this book. First, I would like to thank all the members of LAprepSoccer. More than a decade later, there are more than 10,000 members who have helped organize high school soccer into a real force in the state. The time and energy expended by so many there have fueled this expansion. Among those who deserve special thanks are Chad Vidrine, Floyd Yount, Kathleen Garey, Jay Honoré, Jonathan Rednour, Brother Tim Coldwell, Brian Hall, Jason Oertling, Walter Broussard, Yoshinori Kamo, Ray Linton, Larry Chambless, James Inman, Sean Esker, Paul Malinich, Jeremy Poklemba, Doug Hamilton, and graphic designer, Andres Lugo.

I would also like to thank all of my former soccer teammates and coaches, from Lafreniere to Ridgewood to LSU, especially Coach Eric Anderson, Bryan Fillette, and my brother, Andrew. I am also grateful to some of my friends with whom I watched many games, especially

LAprepSoccer's first graphic designer, Sean Patrick Dempsey Marx, and Ashton and Brendon Oldendorf. Are you Foudious?

There are other friends and teachers who have influenced me in special ways, telling me to write more (Leo Webb, Anne Swan, and Fraser Aitken, whose love of the sport is matched only by his love of Presbytery meetings). Others pushed me to think critically and thoughtfully about the world (Richard Britson, Stuart Irvine, John Whittaker, the late Diogenes Allen, Freida Harris, Lawrence Powell, and James Foster). Many thanks to my parents, Mom, Papa, and Carol, and grandparents for their support and for introducing me to the game. Finally and most importantly, thank you to my greatest source of encouragement and friendship, my wife, Holly. Without your support and understanding, I would never have considered writing any of these words. May we always be lost in wonder, love, and praise.

Scott Crawford
New Orleans
May 2013

Timeline of Soccer in Louisiana

1858 - "Footballs" is offered at the Grand German Volksfest in New Orleans.

1859 – Jefferson City Football Club plays first organized soccer game in New Orleans.

1861 - Soldiers from north Louisiana play soccer at a Confederate camp in Arkansas.

1868 - Day-long Sunday festivals in New Orleans begin regularly to include soccer. St. Joseph's Catholic Church sponsors a team.

1870: New Orleans Lone Star Baseball Football Club and Robert E. Lee Baseball Football Club organize.

1870: The Hibernians of New Orleans start a team.

1873: Louisiana Football Club begins.

1875 - Soccer is the most popular ball sport in New Orleans.

1876 - Ancient Order of Hibernians promotes soccer in New Orleans' Irish neighborhoods.

1877 – Joining the Irish Hibernians are two more New Orleans teams: the Americans and the Englishmen.

1883: New Orleans Football Club begins.

1884: Two more New Orleans teams form: the Bernards and the Hunters.

1886: Louisiana and West End Rowing Clubs play soccer on the banks of Bayou St. John in New Orleans.

1893 - Irish soccer league in New Orleans hosts last game between Faugh a Ballagh and Erin Go Bragh.

1895 - Soccer is introduced at the Young Men's Gymnastics Club.

1895 - Collegiate soccer begins in New Orleans with Tulane, Soule Business College, and Loyola fielding teams.

1896 - Soccer in New Orleans is sometimes held at Athletic Park, the nicest sports field in the state.

1897 - The New Orleans Association Football League begins.

1905 - American football is nearly banned from college campuses.

1905 - Holy Cross defeats Sacred Heart School 1-0 in the first known high school game in Louisiana.

1907 - The New Orleans Association Football League splits from the amateurs and becomes a professional league.

1907 – The first international match in Louisiana history takes place between the local St. Andrews team and the Liverpool Ramblers (England).

1908 - The New Orleans Association Football League folds, but not before sending several players to play professionally in Great Britain.

1912 - The Louisiana Industrial Institute, later named Louisiana Tech, fields a soccer team.

1919 - The first documented game of dock soccer in Louisiana takes place in New Orleans.

1923 - Latin American soccer is organized in New Orleans with the founding of the Guatemala Soccer Club and the New Orleans Soccer Club.

1923 - Honduran-born Carlos Ross Mitchell moves to Louisiana.

1924 - The YWCA plays the first girls soccer game in Louisiana history.

1924 - LSU starts a soccer team.

1924 - The first soccer-specific field is built in Audubon Park, New Orleans.

1930 - The first World Cup is played. The United States finishes third.

1934 - F. C. Germania organizes under the auspices of the Deutsches Haus in New Orleans.

1936 - Latino Tigers organize.

1937 – Women begin playing soccer at Newcomb College in New Orleans.

1938 - 5,000 attend a game in Tad Gormley Stadium between a combined squad of Germania and the Latino Tigers and a Dutch ship.

1938 - The first high school girls teams form at Ursuline Academy.

1947 - Members of F.C. Germania and the Latino Tigers form the International Soccer Ball Club.

1949 - International Soccer Ball Club becomes the New Orleans Soccer Club.

1952 - LSU's team plays games in Tiger Stadium and hosts Penn State, the nation's top program.

1953 - The New Orleans Soccer Club becomes Regal Soccer Club. The club goes 320-4 during a three year run.

1953 - The Gulf Coast Soccer League is formed. Charter members include Tulane, LSU, Regal Soccer Club, Fortier High, and F.C. Germania.

1955 - First interscholastic soccer game since 1905 is played between Fortier and Country Day. Fortier wins 2-0.

1959 – Carlos Ross Mitchell founds Honduras Soccer Club.

1960 – Soccer appears in Lafayette for the first time when the University of Southwestern Louisiana (ULL) fields a club soccer team.

1963 - The Gulf Coast Soccer League is renamed the International Soccer League of New Orleans (ISLANO). ISLANO continues to this day.

1963 - Soccer arrives in Hammond. The Hammond Lions and Tulane join ISLANO.

1966 - Olympia Soccer Club, youth and adults teams of mostly Hondurans, starts.

1966 - The original Louisiana Soccer Association begins under the direction of Carlos Ross Mitchell.

1967 - New Orleans is promised a North American Soccer League (NASL) franchise. However, no team is awarded.

1967 – The LSU men's club team travels to Nicaragua to play the University of Central American and the Yucatan All Stars. Louisiana Governor, John McKeithen, and LSU President, John Hunter, travel with the team.

1968 - Brother Alphonse LeBlanc establishes the Interscholastic Junior Soccer League (IJSL) with the help of Dave "Pro" Scheuermann and Carlos Mitchell.

1968 - The Greater New Orleans Interscholastic Soccer Football League (GNOISFL) replaces the IJSL in the Autumn of 1968.

1969 - Olympia defeats Holy Cross in the first GNOISFL championship during the Spring.

1969 - Pan American Stadium is built in City Park, thanks to the efforts of the LSA. It is the first soccer-specific stadium in Louisiana.

1971 - The New Orleans Interscholastic Soccer League (NOISL) replaces the GNOISFL.

1972 - U.S. Congress passes Title IX, which forbids discrimination in schools based on gender.

1974 – Lafreniere Soccer Club begins in Metairie.

1975 – The Baton Rouge Soccer Association begins.

1975 – Tulane's men's team defeats Georgia Tech in the Finals of the SEC Soccer Classic in Atlanta.

1976 – The Slidell Youth Soccer Club begins.

1976 – SUNS, a precursor to the Carrollton Soccer Association, begins. Organized by Miles Kehoe, Ormonde Plater, and Mike Turner, the club fields a girls team.

1976 – Plantation Athletic Club (PAC) in Algiers and the Latin team, Vita, field girls teams.

1976 - Tulane fields first women's club team.

1976 - University of New Orleans (UNO) field varsity men's program with Coach Gerry Mueller.

1977 - Olympia youth team travels to Philadelphia. Advances to the national youth quarterfinals.

1977 - Interscholastic girls soccer begins in New Orleans with O. Perry Walker, St. Martin's, Country Day, and McGehee.

1978 – The Lafayette Youth Soccer Association begins.

1980 - Interscholastic girls soccer joins the NOISL. There are eight teams.

1980 – The Northeast Louisiana Soccer Association begins.

1982 - The Louisiana Interscholastic Soccer Association (LISA) replaces the NOISL.

1982 - A group in New Orleans nearly buys the Portland Timbers, but the Timbers go bankrupt.

1982 – The St. Charles Soccer Club begins.

1982 – The Covington Youth Soccer Association begins.

1983 – Louisiana Soccer Football Association, the state administrative body, brings USSFA Region III tournament to UNO. Tidewater of New Orleans places third in the women's open division. The Greek-American Soccer Club of New Orleans wins the men's open division, advancing to the Nationals in Dallas.

1984 - Warren Easton makes last appearance in state championship.

1985 - The modern Louisiana Soccer Association is officially incorporated.

1986 - The Louisiana High School Athletic Association (LHSAA) recognizes both boys and girls soccer as varsity sports.

1987 – The Natchitoches Youth Soccer League begins.

1988 - Ganus player Melanie Dube wins court case against the LHSAA allowing her to play on a boys team.

1989 - High school boys participation is great enough to warrant splitting into two divisions.

1989 – The Ascension Area Soccer Association begins.

1990 - International coach, Franz Van Balkom, starts the FVB soccer academy in New Orleans.

1990 – Catholic of Baton Rouge becomes the first team from outside the New Orleans Metro area to win the boys state championship.

1991 - The United Jaguars of Baton Rouge, led by Jason Kreis, win Region III and reach the Finals of the National Youth Challenge Cup.

1993 - Professional soccer returns to New Orleans with the birth of the Riverboat Gamblers. Donnie Pate owns the club. Eleven future MLS players, including Jason Kreis and Stern John, play for the Gamblers.

1993 - Former Hermann Award winner Mike Jeffries becomes director of coaching at Lafreniere.

1993 - The Louisiana High School Soccer Coaches Association (LHSSCA) begins under the direction of Gerald "Gerry" Mueller.

1993 – Tulane men's club team wins the SEC club championship.

1993 - New Orleans Co-Ed Soccer begins.

1993 – Comeaux becomes the first girls team outside the New Orleans Metro area to win state.

1994 – The U.S. hosts the World Cup before record crowds. America advances to the round of sixteen, losing 1-0 to eventual champions Brazil.

1994 - Members of the LSU girls club team succeed in federal lawsuit against the LSU Athletic Department seeking to start a varsity team.

1994 – The New Orleans Soccer Academy grows from FVB.

1994 – The Mandeville Soccer Club begins.

1994 – Alexandria's Crossroads Soccer Association begins.

1995 – Baton Rouge High's Jenny Streiffer Mascaro sets state records in career goals (90) and assists (69).

1995 - LSU fields first varsity women's team.

1995 - Southeastern Louisiana University (SLU) fields varsity women's team.

1995 - High school boys split into three divisions. High school girls split into two divisions.

1995 – The Lafreniere Gamblers '78 boys win the Region III championship and advance to the National Finals.

1996 – Major League Soccer (MLS) begins.

1996 - The Gamblers host the U-23 U.S. Men's National Team. The game ends in a 1-1 tie in front of 11,876 at Tad Gormley Stadium.

1996 - Tulane fields first varsity women's team. Program closes after Katrina and does not restart as of 2013.

1996 - McNeese State University fields first varsity women's team.

1996 – Byrd becomes the first north Louisiana team to win state in girls soccer. Loyola also wins the boys championship, another first for north Louisiana.

1996 – Calcasieu Soccer Club begins.

1997 - Rob Couhig, owner of the Zephyrs minor league baseball team, buys the Gamblers and renames them the Storm. The Storm fold in 2000.

1997 – The Lafayette Swampcats and the Baton Rouge Bombers represent the first professional soccer teams outside New Orleans. They are part of the Eastern Indoor Soccer League, which folded after two seasons.

1998 – The U.S. Open Cup semifinals are played at Zephyr Field in Metairie. 6,154 people watch the Columbus Crew play the New York MetroStars and the Dallas Burn play the Chicago Fire.

1998 - LSU men's club team wins NIRSA National Championship.

1999 – Baton Rouge High's Jenny Streiffer Mascaro becomes a two-time NSCAA All-American at Notre Dame. She later starred for the U.S. Olympics and National teams.

1999 - Scott Crawford creates a website that becomes LAprepSoccer.net, the online soccer community for Louisiana.

1999 - The University of Louisiana Monroe (ULM) fields a varsity women's team.

1999 – The U.S. Women's National Team defeats China in the Women's World Cup. It is the most viewed soccer game in American history.

2000 - The University of Louisiana Lafayette (ULL) fields a varsity women's team.

2000 - Brother Martin defeats Jesuit in the state championship in front of 5,000 viewers at Pan American Stadium. It is one of the largest soccer crowd in Louisiana since 1938 and signals the end of high school championships at Pan American due to capacity concerns.

2001 - High school girls split into three divisions.

2001 – Lafayette Futbol Club begins.

2002 – The U.S. loses 1-0 on a controversial goal to Germany in the Quarterfinals of the World Cup.

2002 – The Iberia Soccer Association begins.

2002 - Dallas Burn beat the real Olympia Club from Honduras in penalty kicks in New Orleans.

2002 – St. Amant's Jason Garey scores 73 goals in a season, bringing his career total to 170. Both are Louisiana high school records.

2003 – The U.S. Women's National Team defeats Brazil 1-0 at Tad Gormley. More than 15,000 attend the biggest game in Louisiana soccer history.

2003 - The New Orleans Shell Shockers of the semi-pro Premier Development League (PDL) begins play. In 2008, they become the Shockers. In 2009, the team changes its name to the Jesters. Attendance never matches that of the Storm and Gamblers.

2005 - Former St. Amant player Jason Garey wins Hermann Award at Maryland.

2006 - Former St. Louis Catholic player Joseph Lapira wins Hermann Award at Notre Dame.

2006 - Lafayette hosts the high school soccer championships as a result of Katrina.

2006 – St. Louis Catholic is ranked #1 in the nation.

2007 – The Baton Rouge Capitals of the Premier Development League (PDL) are founded.

2007 - Shreveport wins bid to host the high school soccer championships. Shreveport hosts through 2010.

2007 - The Beauregard United Soccer Association begins.

2008 - High school playoff brackets change from district-based seeding system to a seeding system based on the votes of coaches. A power rating formula that Yoshinori Kamo developed allows the switch to work.

2009 - High school soccer organizes first All-Star game in July of each year.

2009 – Jesuit is ranked #1 in the nation by ESPN.

2010 – The Chicago Fire Juniors consolidate premier club soccer in New Orleans into one club.

2010 – Sulphur Soccer Club begins.

2011 – Moss Bluff Soccer Club in Lake Charles begins.

2011 – Capital City United in Baton Rouge begins.

2011 - The high school championships return to New Orleans. A crowd of over 6,000 watches St. Paul's snap Jesuit's 95 game unbeaten streak. By 2013, over 10,000 view the high school championships in Tad Gormley Stadium.

2011 – Honduran professional club, Motagua, plays two summer friendlies in Tad Gormley Stadium. The first, against Honduran rival, Olimpia, drew 8,000. The second, against Mexico City's Club America, drew a disappointing 2,500 as a result of Tropical Storm Lee.

2012 – The Louisiana Legislature gives approval to build Heitmeier Soccer Stadium, a 9,000-seat soccer-specific stadium in Algiers with a price tag of twelve million dollars.

2012 - All three divisions in high school play championships together.

2012 - Former Jesuit player Patrick Mullins wins Hermann Award at Maryland.

2012 - LSU men's club team wins Regionals and advances to the NIRSA NCCS National Soccer Championships.

2013 – Mandeville's Delaney Sheehan sets girls high school state records for most goals in a career (201) and most goals in a season (56).

2013 – Jason Oertling of St. Louis Catholic becomes the first high school coach to win ten state championships. St. Louis also becomes the first boys program to win four championships in a row since Warren Easton.

2013 – Tooraj Badie of Sacred Heart becomes the first high school girls coach to win six championships. Badie also was named High School Player of the Year in 1982 before playing for the UNO men's team.

2013 – The Women's Professional Indoor Soccer League begins with the semi-pro Baton Rouge Charm and New Orleans Creole Ladies.

2013 – The NOLA Soccer Academy, connected to the N.O. Jesters, begins.

2013 – LA Fire U16 Navy team wins the Region III girls championship. They are the first Louisiana girls club to win a regional championship.

1858-1895:
Immigrant football

Soccer is fondly referred to as the beautiful game. What makes it beautiful is its simplicity. The game is not burdened by a long, complicated list of arbitrary rules. If soccer were to change this, it would cease to be soccer. Soccer has always been simple, even in the beginning. In the middle of the nineteenth century soccer existed as a game throughout several European nations, their colonies, and in America and Canada.

This game had origins in human nature: people enjoy playing games that engage their mind, body, and community. Humans enjoy setting goals and achieving excellence. It is part of our DNA; it is how we were designed and created. Humans have been playing games similar to soccer for millennia. The Chinese had the first documented soccer-like game, *cuju*, dating to the third century BC. The Japanese played *kemari*. The Greeks and Romans played *phaininda* and *harpastum*, respectively. The Mayans painted murals of men kicking a ball. The Australian Aboriginals played *Woggabaliri*. "Mob football" amongst rival towns was a staple in medieval England that eventually evolved into the modern game.

All through these varying names, the idea behind the many names of soccer was simple. There were two teams. There were goal posts. Goals were scored kicking a ball. In the middle of the nineteenth century the game became more and more popular, thanks largely to the effects of the Industrial Revolution, which will be discussed below.

The game became more defined as well. As a result, different forms of the sport started springing forth. From the simplicity of soccer, the more complex games of rugby and American football would be born. This divergence of several sports from one and the resulting shared nomenclature make tracing the origins of the sport difficult.

What's in a Name?

In the 1850s in America, the term *football* had two meanings. First, it was most commonly used as a term of political derision. Today, we might say "punching bag." Then, if a writer wanted to express that someone or something was being taken advantage of or kicked around, the writer would write that person or thing was a "football."

The second meaning of *football* during that time period has little to do with the modern game of American football, which did not exist at the time. What did exist in New Orleans and many American port cities in the middle of the nineteenth century was a game called football, a close parent of modern soccer. The rules changed ever so slightly and were refined, but the *football* discussed in New Orleans in the 1850s to the 1880s is what we today call soccer. By the 1890s, soccer in Louisiana was known by at least six different names: *association football, football, Irish football, soccer, socker,* and *football soccer.*

Incidentally, the term *soccer* comes from a practice at Oxford University in the mid-1800s of referring to people in clubs using the club's name suffixed with the letters "er". At that time at Oxford, soccer was called *association football*. Thus, athletes who played association football were called *assocers*. Eventually, this term was shortened to *soccer*.

In Louisiana, *football* was the preferred name of the sport from its beginning in the 1850s to the 1880s. In the 1880s, *association football* gained wide usage, and continued to be the word of choice through the 1930s.

By the mid 1900s, the many names of soccer were reduced to two: *soccer* and *soccer football*. American football had quickly placed the term *football* under its bailiwick, thanks to its meteoric rise in popularity at the turn of the century. The preferred term in Louisiana for most of the twentieth century was *soccer football*. In fact, the name *soccer football* lasted into the 1980s. Serving as just one example of this now outdated terminology was high school soccer. The first modern varsity soccer league in Louisiana, which began in the Autumn of 1968, was named the Greater New Orleans Interscholastic Soccer Football League. By the mid-1970s, the term *soccer* was the preferred term in America and in Louisiana.

In the beginning.

On May 17, 1858, the city of New Orleans stood on pins and needles. The Mississippi River was nearing its Spring crest. Each year, the Father of Waters rose and rose, as melting snow and Spring rains from much of the North American continent collected in that shunt that leads to the Gulf of Mexico. Levees had been built up and down the river to protect sugar cane plantations that drove the economic engine of southern Louisiana. The levees near New Orleans were especially tall and wide. Were they wide and tall enough?

Those levees withstood the battering river's torrent, most of the time at least. In the city's hundred or so years of river levee fortification, the levees had failed and the city flooded on only five occasions: 1785, 1791, 1799, 1816, and 1849. Would 1858 be added to the list?

On April 11, 1858 the levee two miles upriver at Bell's plantation broke. It was a large crevasse, but it did not endanger New Orleans. The crevasse was on the other side of the river, the west or left bank, while New Orleans sits on the east or right bank. The failure of the levee was actually good news for the city, as it gave the river an outlet, and thus eased the pressure on the levees near the city.

Five weeks later, on May 17, the people of New Orleans woke to the news that the levee on the east bank above the city had failed. It was at La Branche, near Destrehan, where 47 years earlier, Charles Deslonde led an army of 500 slaves in the largest slave revolt in American history, that the levee broke. As the water gushed towards Lake Pontchartrain, the collective blood pressure of the city jumped. Was a rush of water coming to inundate the Crescent City?

The worry was only shortly lived. The water did not snake its way into the city. It flowed to the lake and out the Rigolets into the Gulf. The city was spared, and so the people could get back to the amusement season that was soon coming to a close.

From mid-May through early October, New Orleans can be an unbearable place. High temperatures combined with high humidity can push the heat index above 110. During the doldrums of August, when a storm is not brewing, lows often do not dip below 80 degrees. In a time before air condition, and with the constant threat of a yellow fever outbreak, the summer was a time in which people with means left. Those without means prayed that they would survive the summer.

The rest of the year was festival time. Those living in cold climes come to life in the summer. In New Orleans, life bloomed in the winter and early spring. The opera, the ballet, concerts, balls, and church and civic festivals were all part of the amusement season. May 17 was the festival season's finale.

One group that loved festivals was the German Americans, and in 1858, there were plenty of German Americans in New Orleans. The period from 1830 to 1860 saw an enormous influx of Germans to the region. The number one port of entry in the States was New York. New Orleans was second. The reason for New Orleans' lofty standing was the cotton trade.

1850s New Orleans was the cotton capital of the world. The city was a hundred miles from the nearest cotton plantations, but the city was responsible for financing almost all cotton plantations in the South. As a result, New Orleans became the banking and export capital of the South, and one of the most important economic engines in the world. Much of the cotton that left New Orleans was destined to Le Havre, France. Le Havre, located on the English Channel, was the center of the Continental cotton exchange.

Ships arrived in Le Havre filled with bale after bale of cotton. Unloaded, those ships needed ballast for the return trip. But rather than return with cobblestones that line many of the streets in Uptown New Orleans, in the 1830s, the ships began to return with Germans. Most of these early Germans were peasants, fleeing their native land due to the ravages that the Napoleonic Wars had on southern Germany.

In the late 1840s, however, educated middle class Germans began appearing in Louisiana. Persecution forced these Germans from their homes. In 1848, much of the German middle class was exhausted by the aristocratic rule of the many German states. The middle class wanted more freedom, more control, and most importantly, a united German nation. Hoping to achieve these goals, they staged a revolution. Squashed by the ruling aristocrats and their revolution a failure, these Germans fled the aristocrats' retribution.

Meanwhile, America was quickly growing. Its economy was booming. The Western frontier was open. Free and cheap land was to be had for those with a heart of adventure. Freedom and fortunes were there for the taking. For well-educated German refugees, America was a land flowing with milk and honey.

The proximity of Germany to Le Havre, where easy and cheap passage was available, made the trans-Atlantic crossing a viable choice. And cross the Germans did. This wave of immigration was mostly Protestant, with about a third Catholic, and about 250,000 German Jews.

During the 1850s, tens of thousands of German arrived in New Orleans yearly. In 1853 alone, more than 50,000 Germans saw for the first time that famous crescent in the river. Many kept moving, ending up in the Mississippi, Missouri, and Ohio River valleys. However, a sizeable chunk of Germans settled in New Orleans, making the city a cultural hub for German Americans. Many German civic organizations formed to help the newly arrived Germans acclimate to the new nation and allow those already in Louisiana to preserve their German culture.

One of the highlights of the German American calendar was the Grand German Volksfest. Each year, several of the biggest German American organizations in New Orleans gathered on Canal Street. The groups snaked their way through the French Quarter to Esplanade

Avenue. Up Esplanade they went before ending at Union Course, a horse track located today where the Fair Grounds in Gentilly is located.

At the Union Course, a host of outdoor activities was on offer. Building and strengthening the German community was the goal of the Grand Volksfest. Event planners hoped that the many games would attract the German masses. One of those games was "Footballs," as described in the below newspaper advertisement for the festival.

This advertisement for the Volksfest is the first known mention of the game of footballs, or soccer, in Louisiana history. In fact, it is the first known mention of football, which was closer to today's soccer than today's football, in the South, and one of the first mentions of the sport in all of America. It may not have been modern soccer as we know it, but it was a close relative and forerunner of the game we know today.

The German Americans, however, did not bring the sport from their homeland. Soccer did not exist in Germany until 1874 when an Englishman introduced the sport to Dresden. The Germans were slow to adopt the sport as well, and soccer did not become popular in the Rhineland until the 1890s. So how did it appear in 1858 in German New Orleans? Perhaps a few of the immigrants picked up the game from an English or Scotsman who was stationed in Le Havre. Or perhaps English or Scotsmen living in New Orleans had already popularized the game among locals when this advertisement was published. Both New Orleans and Le Havre were cosmopolitan port cities that had direct contact with England and Scotland, the birthplace of modern soccer. That the advertisement for footballs included no explanation about what the game was indicates that the sport was already known, yet not reported, in the city.

The Grand German Volksfest
Will be continued and concluded
On SUNDAY, the 16th, and MONDAY, 17th May, 1858.

The Procession will be formed at 9 o'clock A. M., on Canal street, proceed through St. Charles street, Poydras to Camp, Chartres, St. Louis to Royal, and through Esplanade to the Union Course, where, after a short rest, the following festivities and sports will take place.

Bird and Target Shooting, Gymnastical Exercises, Race and Sackrunning, Mastclimbing, Footballs, Sports on Horseback, and Songs executed by the German Singers, under the direction of Mr. H. F. Brand

Thirty-six Musicians will accompany the procession and execute Concert and Dancing Music on the ground.

Admission for gentlemen, $1; ladies and children free.

Mr. T. B. Simmson & Co.'s Bayou Road omnibuses will run all day in such short intervals as necessity may dictate, at the regular fare.

The Daily Picayune, May 16, 1858.

Soccer's beginning in Louisiana received no post-event fanfare. There would be no more soccer games in New Orleans that summer. A major yellow fever epidemic was about to strike the city. Soccer was the last thing on peoples' minds.

As the first cool fronts pushed through southeastern Louisiana in October and November, joy returned to life. The coolness allowed the pace of life to quicken. Festival and games season would soon be upon the city.

Soccer reappeared in January of 1859. While footballs was already known and offered, at least at the German Volksfest, an actual game of soccer was not documented. That changed on January 25, 1859. The previous day, the first documented game of soccer in Louisiana was played. This document does not come to us in the form of a game program, box score, or a league advertisement. It comes from a New Orleans police report. In this less than proud beginning for the local game, four young men were arrested for "playing football on Sunday; also for being complained of as a nuisance to the neighborhood." The ban against public games in New Orleans on Sunday only existed the city's Protestant neighborhoods. This was a vestige of a Calvinist tradition that existed in Scotland and England, where a forerunner to soccer was banned on the Sabbath all the way back to the seventeenth century.

When brought before the Court, the four pioneers of the local sport gave a simple defense: the entire neighborhood was involved in the game. They scattered when the police came. Why arrest us alone? The judge, impressed with the defense, dismissed the charges and let the men go on their way.

Standing behind that reasoning for arrest, though, was that of an epidemic. New Orleans, due to its geography, weather, and very compact urbanized area, was a hotbed for epidemics of yellow fever throughout the 1800s. Spread by the mosquito *Aedes aegypti*, the RNA virus known as yellow fever made an annual appearance in New Orleans until 1905. People did not wonder if the outbreak would happen; it was inevitable. People wondered how bad the outbreak would be.

In 1819, an outbreak killed 2200 when the city's population was just 50,000. In 1853, an outbreak killed nearly 8,000. When those four arrested boys were arrested, New Orleans was from a summer of yellow fever that killed 4,845. Even though it was winter and the mosquito population diminished, the memory of that summer lingered in the minds of some in the neighborhood. Public assemblies that disturbed the mud streets caused miasmas, poisonous, yellow fever-laden vapors released from the ground. Or so some of the neighbors incorrectly thought. They summoned the police and one of the first recorded soccer games in Louisiana came to an end.

> **Police Matters.**
>
> RECORDER SUMMERS' COURT.—Four young men, who were arrested yesterday, were presented to the Recorder by some policemen for "playing football on Sunday; also for being complained of as a nuisance to the neighborhood." The defendants didn't deny an impromptu game of football, but alleged that the neighbors took a hand in it themselves. As the "neighborhood" didn't appear in court to bear out the allegation of the policemen, and as no harm resulted—though streets are no places for such amusement—and there being no "blue law" amongst our ordinances, the Recorder very properly discharged the parties.

The Daily True Delta, January 25, 1859.

The New Orleans neighborhood in which this game was played is unknown. It may have taken place in the Irish Channel, between the Garden District and the Mississippi River. It could have taken place in what became known as Little Saxony, an area just downriver of the French Quarter in what is today called Marigny. Or it may have occurred just upriver of the Garden District, in Jefferson City.

It was in this sliver by the river that many German and Irish immigrants lived in the mid and late-1800s. In this narrow strip of land, later dubbed "the tea kettle," immigrants found their home. This land was desirable – it was far enough away from the River to avoid most of the nuisances associated with a major port. It was also on high ground, important in a city near sea level that faced the threat of deluge by both river and sea. The land was also affordable – unlike the homes on St. Charles and Esplanade Avenues, where wealthy English and Scottish

33

Protestants, descendants of the "Kantucks" who came in droves a generation earlier, and French Creole Catholics settled, respectively. German and Irish immigrants flocked to the city and to these neighborhoods in particular. These dirty, narrow streets near the river birthed and cradled soccer in Louisiana.

Though the exact location and identities of the players of the first recorded game of soccer in Louisiana are not known, we do know that the city's first organized football team was Irish. This team, the Jefferson City Football Club (JCFC), organized in 1859. Jefferson City at that time was part of Jefferson Parish and was a town in its own right. Its main intersection was Jefferson Avenue and Magazine Street, in what today is one of New Orleans' most tony neighborhoods. At that time, however, most residents were Irish Catholic immigrants who lived in modest shotguns spaced closely together with unpaved, dirty streets in front.

This first team of Irish players from this neighborhood did not just want to play; they also wanted an audience. "Players issued special invitations asking ladies to be present for their games" (Somers, Dale A. *The Rise of Sports in New Orleans: 1850-1900*. And come they did. Crowds gathered for some of JCFC's first games against ragtag bunches of players in the neighborhood.

The 1858 origin of Louisiana soccer is noteworthy. That long ago date makes Louisiana one of the first American states where soccer appeared. Indeed, it was one of the first places in the world that soccer appeared, predating all non-British nations, including France, Italy, Spain, and Brazil. To put that date in context, the first documented game in St. Louis, the capital of American soccer throughout much of the 1900s, was

1859, and St. Louis did not start organized soccer until 1875. Modern soccer did not come to France until 1863, Italy in 1887, and Brazil in 1894. That 1858 origin allows Louisiana to claim a very special place in the history of international soccer.

When soccer first appeared in Louisiana, there were very few places in the world where soccer existed. Internationally, the only countries that played the sport were Scotland, the United States, and England. Within the United States, very few cities knew soccer in 1858. Only Boston (1843), Exeter, New Hampshire (1845), and New York City (1845) predate New Orleans. Two colleges, Harvard and Dartmouth (1855), and a graduate school, Princeton Theological Seminary (1856), have soccer histories that predate New Orleans soccer.

Soccer's earliest beginnings in Louisiana had a simple origin. Like the game is played still in many parts of the world, in 1858 New Orleans, soccer was part of the festival and street scene. It was a game played amongst neighborhood residents likely seeking a taste of athletic diversion and fun. New Orleans was not unique in this regard: two American port cities had similar soccer-like football street games. These games might have been quite organic in nature -- a few fellows find a ball and start kicking it or it may have shown a spread of the game from the United Kingdom, where such games existed dating back medieval times. Modern Association Football, though, started in 1840s Britain. The sport formally organized and codified its rules in 1863. These rules took about two decades to reach New Orleans.

The beginning of organized soccer in Louisiana cannot be understood apart from the socio-economic soil from which it grew. The 1850s was a pivotal decade in the United States. America was growing rapidly, but perhaps more significant than its numerical growth was the new distribution of the United States' population. From the birth of the nation until 1850, the vast majority of Americans, around 90%, lived a rural, agrarian life. The economic and cultural institutions reflected and contributed form to that life. Americans farmed, raised livestock, and lived geographically secluded lives.

The effects of the Industrial Revolution rapidly revolutionized how Americans lived. Beginning in 1850, there was a rapid rise in the percentage of Americans living in urban areas. Looking only at Louisiana, in 1850, Louisiana had 518,000 residents. New Orleans had 116,000 residents, representing 22% of the state's population, the same proportion in 1810. By 1900, that proportion rose to 26%. The rise in percentage was not greater only because city populations in Shreveport, Baton Rouge, Alexandria, Monroe, and Lafayette also saw growth, drawing rural residents to the cities. Louisiana, one of the most rural of American states, became a much more urbanized state beginning in 1850.

Six-day work weeks were the norm in this newly developing American urban culture. On the seventh day, most went to church. After church, Catholics and German Protestants engaged in recreational activities. Anglo-Saxon Protestants rested. But the Anglo-Saxon Protestants, despite attempts by several ministers to popularize a Sabbath Observance League, soon acquiesced to the New Orleans Creole culture of recreation on Sunday.

But what forms of recreations were there in New Orleans during this time? Sport in America, as it was in Europe, traditionally was a hobby of hunting, fishing, horse riding, and animal fighting. Urbanization changed that.

New to cities, most city dwellers, even in an island city like New Orleans, did not have the option to head to the local fishing holes or the woods. New types of recreation that fit the urban context of the 1850s developed in Europe and America. Among the most popular of these games were rugby, cricket, baseball, association football (soccer), and American football. All of these games were based on ancient sports and the games were not highly differentiated from each other. Soon, however, the urban sports lovers created rigidly codified institutions representing these sports.

Cities grew, usually without much planning. The result was a highly unorganized, dirty, and unpleasant place to live. City planners recognized the inhumane living conditions many faced. To ameliorate this problem, city leaders across America went on public health campaigns and sought to build public parks.

In New Orleans, City Park was officially set aside in 1854, although it existed on maps as the "city park" at least a decade earlier, and Audubon Park in 1871. These and other open, green spaces moved urbanized sport from the dirty mud streets of the city to playing fields we recognize today.

Just before the Civil War, sport was a cornerstone of American life for the first time in the nation's history. Americans, seeking to escape the drudgery of factory labor, working port docks, and other soul destroying labor, turned to sport to give them meaning and escape. Following the Civil War, Americans resumed their love and passion for sport. When labor movements helped ensure shorter working hours and higher pay, recreational and professional sports grew enormously in Europe and America.

During the Civil War, however, sports did exist. Most often, they existed in army camps. It is wrong to think of the Civil War as a continuous battle. There were many battles during those four years, but there were also many lulls in the barbarism of war. During these lulls, sports were a welcome diversion.

Camp Jackson was a Confederate stronghold in 1861. Located at the very northwestern tip of Arkansas in Benton County, it is not where one would expect Louisiana soccer to have roots. But it was there, in that army camp, that one reporter witnessed several Louisiana men playing, in his words, "the most animated game of foot-ball I ever beheld." What we can note is that he obviously had seen other games of football, likely in Louisiana, since he was from the Bayou State.

More importantly, though, is noting the homes of these soldier-players. New Orleans has been the center of Louisiana soccer in modern times. Most state championships come from the city. More people in the New Orleans Metro area play soccer than in any other area of the state. As a result, much of the history of Louisiana soccer focuses on New Orleans.

The Confederates who played in that Camp Jackson game, however, were not from New Orleans. They were, in fact, from northern Louisiana. Captain Gilmore of Shreveport, Captain Viglint of the Pelican Rifles (from DeSoto and Natchitoches Parishes), Lieutenant Bursh Wolway, and Captain Gunnels of the Caldwell Guards (from Caldwell Parish in north central Louisiana) were among the first known soccer players from Louisiana.

What makes it likely that this game was more soccer-like than rugby-like is the use of the term *football* and the description of Captain Gunnels standing "way back in the rear, dignified," as though he were standing guard of the goal, as a modern day goal keeper does.

> This evening I witnessed the most animated game of foot-ball I ever beheld. Foremost among the combatants were Capt. Gilmore, of the Shreveport Rangers; Capt. Viglini, Pelican Rifles; Lieut. Bursh Wolway, Adjutant Hyams, Sergeant-Major Third regiment Louisiana volunteers, and way back in the rear, dignified, or more classically, "grand, gloomy and peculiar," stood Capt. Gunnels, of the Caldwell Guards.
>
> Really it was a magnificent sight. The Louisianians playing football! Let Mr. Harper send down his artist and we will give him a scene to paint he never dreamed of. But

The Daily True Delta, October 23, 1861.

What is peculiar about these names and the places from which they came is that they likely were not first generation immigrants. Most north Louisianan white citizens were from Protestant families with English, Scottish, Welsh, or Northern Irish origins. They had arrived on the East Coast in the late eighteenth century, often in the states of Virginia and North Carolina. From there, they moved westward, eventually making their way to northern Louisiana. The etymology of these surnames suggests a similar history.

So then, where does soccer in northern Louisiana come from? The only answer is speculative. It seems the answer will forever be lost to history. The important lesson here, though, is that soccer has as long a history amongst the people of northern Louisiana as southern Louisiana.

The Postbellum years in Louisiana initially did not see much soccer participation. There were occasional games of "football" played at family picnics in New Orleans, but no organized leagues.

1868 brought with it the first public request for soccer players. Much like a message board post or Facebook status update today, this printed request sought players for a pick-up game of the "exhilarating game of football" at the Fair Grounds.

> FOOTBALL PLAYERS, ATTENTION! — We publish elsewhere a request that those amateurs of the exhilarating game of football, who may desire to take part in a friendly set to, will meet at the race course stand of the Fair Grounds this evening at 4 o'clock.

The Daily Picayune, May 8, 1868

Two months later, St. Joseph's Catholic Church, the largest parish in New Orleans at the time, held a fair at Oakland Race Course to benefit the church. Despite inclement weather, "the boys about the grounds, determined to be amused, got up a game of foot-ball, and although it was hard work for them to do justice to this game, on account of the mud, yet they seemed to like it, and the rest of the people were pleased if they were."

> **The Catholic Festival.**
>
> For the benefit of St. Joseph's Church, which has the largest parish in this city, a festival, was organized to take place at the Oakland Race Course, which we regret to say was interrupted by the unpropitious weather. On Sunday a large number of the church parishoners and the public in general thronged the grounds, but it was the understanding that the Grand Festival would be postponed until the coming Sunday, at which time, weather permitting, a grand affair may well be anticipated.
>
> The Festival on Sunday labored under the disadvantage of the extremely bad weather, the recent drizzling rains making the grounds about the entrance to the race course muddy and unpleasant. A light breeze, however, served to make the entertainment more happy than it would have been were it not for its influence.
>
> The boys about the grounds, determined to be amused, got up a game of foot-ball, and although it was hard work for them to do justice to this game, on account of the mud, yet they seemed to like it, and the rest of the people were pleased if they were.

The *New Orleans Times*, July 7, 1868

Sporting recreation grew in the post-Civil War years. Catholic and German Protestant churches and civic organizations regularly hosted outdoor festivals that highlighted the new culture of recreation. At another such festival in 1868, "A grand foot-ball match wound up the amusements." Meanwhile, in New Orleans, Anglo-Saxon Protestants focused on a non-sporting form of recreation: Mardi Gras parades.

Soccer in New Orleans seems to have been popular amongst two immigrant populations in the 1860s and into at least the 1870s: the Catholic Irish and the Protestant German communities. The Irish had their own teams. The Germans, at the very least, played the game at their annual Grand German Volksfest. By 1875, the year of St. Louis' first organized soccer game, soccer was the city's most popular ball sport, supplanting an earlier versions of tennis called *games of raquette* (*The Daily Picayune*, May 30, 1875).

During the 1870s and 1880s, the Ancient Order of Hibernians (AOH) was the most well known organization supporting soccer. Originally a secret society of Irish Catholics, the AOH's mission evolved from one of protection from anti-Catholic activities (1830s - 1860s) to that of a social and civic organization (1870s – present). In June of 1876, the New Orleans chapter of the AOH sponsored a match between members of the organizations. Each team had twelve members and the audience was given three barrels of beer (*The Daily Picayune*, June 30, 1876).

The Screwmen's Benevolent Association (SBA) also held an annual festival that included soccer, beginning in 1880. The SBA was a union for dockhands and roustabouts who helped pack bales of cotton into ships. In New Orleans, most of the members of the SBA were Irish. The SBA may represent the forerunners to dock soccer, a brand of soccer played by crews of visiting ships from various nations. Dock soccer receives its own chapter later in the book.

In April of 1880, the SBA held a benefit for the Irish Relief Fund at the Fair Grounds. Besides running races and horse races, the society sponsored a baseball match, a competition of "greasing a pig," climbing a greasy pole, female waltzing, and a "Grand Challenge Football Match" (*The Daily City Item*, April 15, 1880).

The Irish National League was yet another Irish civic group that hosted soccer matches. The organization likewise held its annual festival on the Fair Grounds. Games were similar to other festival games. However, its grand football match was played between "two picked teams, 21 on each side" (*The Daily Picayune*, July 29, 1883).

The transformation of Louisiana soccer from hobby to organized sport had its birth in the Catholic immigrant population in New Orleans. While many groups occasionally played the game of soccer at Sunday festivals, there were very few teams that consistently played the game until the 1890s. It was during that decade that two Irish squads formed: Faugh a Ballagh and Erin Go Bragh. Faugh a Ballagh was led by a diminutive, 100 pound man named Joseph P. Callighan. Meanwhile, Erin Go Bragh's captain, John J. O'Neal, weighed in at 200 pounds.

FOOTBALL.
IRISH TEAMS TO PLAY.
If the weather is fine there will be a genuine Irish football game to-day, with all the accomplishments of shinning and kicking and may the best man win. The game is attracting considerable attention from the players and their friends and the spirit of rivalry is strong between the champions of the different provinces. The teams will be as follows:
Faugh a Ballagh Team—Joseph P. Callighan, captain, 100; John Kilroy 170, Matt. Killilea 180, Martin Dooley 131, Edgar Grogan 140, James Brady 170, Pat Harran 185, Wm. Mitchell 150, Joseph Ward 180, Thomas Mitchell 168, James Cain 100, Mike Caufield 165.
Erin Go Bragh Team—John J. O'Neal captain, 200 pounds; John Ambrose 140, Wm. Cahill 145, John Coleman 145, Wm. Caughlin 140, John Kelly 140, Thomas Fagho 140, John Walsh 155, James Murphy 155, Wm. Nagle 145, John P. Sullivan 180, Tom Ambrose 130.

The Daily Picayune, February 12, 1893

In addition to the German and Irish groups, workers' societies and sporting groups enjoyed soccer matches in New Orleans during Reconstruction. In 1877, the Lafayette Hook and Ladder Company No. 1 and Creole Steam Fire Company No. 9 sponsored a festival at the Fair Grounds in New Orleans. Amongst the sports played was a "football match between the English and American teams" (*The New Orleans Item*, May 13, 1877), followed by a baseball match between the R. E. Lees and the Washingtons. Soccer fever spread to the members of the Louisiana and West End Rowing Clubs, who met to play soccer on

43

the banks of Bayou St. John in August of 1886 (*The Daily Picayune*, August 17, 1886).

By 1887, soccer was well established in German and Irish immigrant communities in New Orleans. It would soon establish a foothold in other communities in New Orleans. Helping lead the cause was *The Daily Picayune*. The daily was one of the leading papers in the South, and published an editorial stating, "Football is recommended for all college students who kick" (*The Daily Picayune, October 2, 1887*). The owner of *The Daily Picayune* during this time was Eliza Jane Nicholson. A lover of animals, Nicholson was a proponent of many sports like soccer because she hoped that these games would supplant another popular pastime in Louisiana at the time: dog fighting.

At the same time of soccer's emergence into nativist communities in New Orleans, American football or gridiron football rapidly became the sport of America. Beginning around 1890, the term *football*, when used in papers in Louisiana, referred to American football, which at that time, was predominantly played by colleges in the Northeast, such as Yale, Rutgers, Princeton, and Harvard.

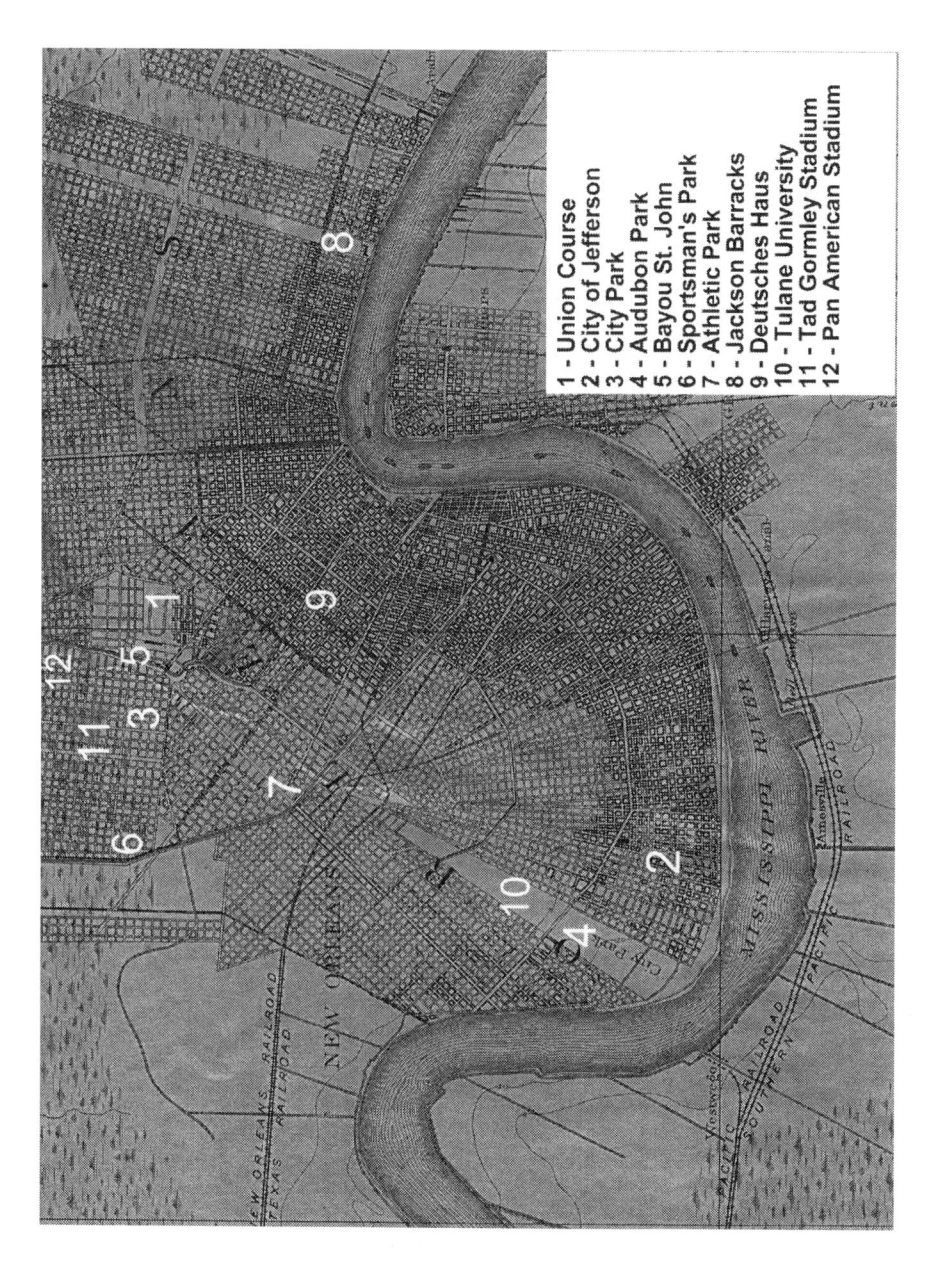

U.S. Geological Survey, 1891

1895-1904:
Association Football and Athletic Clubs

Athletic clubs did not exist in America before the Civil War. That soon changed following the war's conclusion. As rural people moved in mass to urban areas, population density increased rapidly. At the same time, labor unions pushed to shorten the hours laborers worked. Helping the unions gain victory was a boom in technology that increased production while decreasing the need for manual labor. These three factors helped lead to the formation of athletic clubs.

Athletic clubs, though, were elite social institutions in America during this time period. Few working class members joined the exclusive clubs. However, the economic byproduct of the post-Industrial Revolution gave the wealthy more leisure time as well. Many in the upper class joined these athletic clubs because of this new free time.

Some of the earliest athletic clubs in America were northeastern clubs. The New York Athletic Club organized in 1868. Three years later, the Penn Athletic Club began in Philadelphia. Not long thereafter, though, the Young Men's Gymnastic Club in New Orleans was founded in 1872. The YMGC was one of the first athletic clubs in New Orleans and the South, but became the most popular and the longest lasting. Today, the club still exists at 222 North Rampart Street. Visitors can walk its halls and enjoy its equipment for $20 a day.

The gym's doors were not always open to the public. Blacks were not allowed membership until 1986. The gym opened its doors to women only in 1989. In its early years, the Young Men's Gymnastic Club was an elite social club. Its members were comprised mostly of white, wealthy Protestants and a few wealthy Jewish members of Western European origin (The Jews of Eastern Europe that arrived in New Orleans around this time were excluded by the social elite, including Jews already in New Orleans).

Although it is often assumed that Southern white Protestants did not get along with Jews in the South a century ago, that assumption is incorrect. In New Orleans, it could even be said that the elite Protestants, usually Episcopal and Presbyterian, had no closer religious allies than the Western European Jews of New Orleans.

The affinity the elite Protestants of New Orleans shared with the Western European Jews of New Orleans had three root causes. First, Judah Touro, a prominent Jew, supported and built several Episcopal and Presbyterian churches in the early 1800s. Second, Jewish merchants in New Orleans of this period were more likely to support the new American Protestant culture and worldview than the Creole Catholic culture that had dominated, most easily expressed in the historic Batture Case involving Edward Livingston and President Jefferson. Third, New Orleans' early Protestants, and later, the socially elite, were overwhelmingly Episcopal and Presbyterian, as opposed to Lutheran, Methodist, and Baptist in the rest of the South. These Episcopalians and especially Presbyterians had a stronger strain of Augustinian-Calvinist theology, and thus, were more inclined to see Judaism in a positive light than the other branches of Protestantism.

As a result of these and other causes, New Orleans was a socially open place for Western European and especially German Jews in the late 1800s, when the YMGC was trying to promote soccer in the city. As a result, elite social institutions, such as Mardi Gras krewes (the first Rex was Jewish) and social clubs, like the YMGC, were open to Jewish members.

The YMGC was open only to the 1% of New Orleans. In order to gain admittance to the club, a candidate needed three recommendations from existing members, and any potential applicant could be blackballed. As a result, in the early days, few if any Irish or German Catholics were members, despite a membership in the club that exceeded a thousand men.

Soccer in New Orleans was transitioning from an immigrant game to a game embraced and encouraged by the socially elite, which in New Orleans included Jews, Episcopalians, and Presbyterians. During the last week of October of 1895, Professor Whitehouse, one of the leaders of the YMGC, introduced the club to the game of association football.

According to the report, Whitehouse took sixteen men to Sportsman's Park, where "for an hour and a half coached them on the rules and fine points of the association football." The earliest games of the YMGC were held at Sportsman's Park and the Fair Grounds.

FOOTBALL.

ASSOCIATION FOOTBALL.

Prof. Whitehouse, of the Young Men's Gymnastic Club, last Sunday took sixteen men out to Sportsman's park, and for an hour and a half coached them on the rules and fine points of the association football. They were quick to learn, and with the assistance of Welnecke and Burt, both of whom have played the game, Prof. Whitehouse was enabled to give the boys a thorough schooling in the sport.

This Sunday there will be another crowd of men on the grounds playing the game, but the Fair grounds will be substituted for the Sportsman's park, on account of a game of baseball scheduled for that date at the latter place. Prof. Whitehouse is very much encouraged with the day's sport, and feels confident that before long he will have an excellent team to place before the public. He will also try to introduce the game in other clubs.

The Daily Picayune, October 29, 1895.

Sportsman's Park deserves some mention here since it was one of the first locations that soccer was played in a truly organized fashion. The park was located in a center of recreation for New Orleanians. Originally, it was located in the Bayou Metairie area, across from the Metairie Race Course. The racecourse today is the Metairie Cemetery, the famed above-ground landmark visible from the Pontchartrain Expressway.

Sportsman's Park was an open field that developed into an area for baseball and soccer teams to practice and play. In the early 1900s, a famous, and recently demolished, jazz hall, the Halfway House, was built next to Sportsman's Park. Soccer teams continued to play at Sportsman's Park until moving to Heinemann Park in 1915.

College soccer began in Louisiana at the same time that athletic clubs began playing the game. In May of 1895, Tulane, Soule Business College, and Loyola fielded their first teams. Tulane's first opponent was Centenary College, which at this time was located in Jackson, Mississippi. Centenary moved to Shreveport a decade later.

> **FOOTBALL.**
>
> **A JUNIOR GAME CANCELED.**
>
> To-day the football season in New Orleans was to have been formally opened, but owing to the inability of the Tulane freshmen class to secure a competent team the game was canceled. This game was to have been held on the Tulane grounds between a team from the freshman class and the Southern Athletic Club's junior eleven. Some four weeks ago a number of the young boys of the Southern Club met and organized a team, and Sidney Lehlemann was made the captain. They arranged a game with the Tulanes for to-day, and a game with Soule's school team and the Jesuits for later dates. A day or two ago the manager of the Tulane team notified the Southerns that it would be impossible to secure a suitable eleven, and the game was canceled. However, on next Saturday there will be a game between the Tulane University team and a team from the Centenary College of Jackson, Miss.

The Daily Picayune, November 6, 1895.

Athletic club soccer was on the rise in the mid and late 1890s in New Orleans. Joining the YMGC soccer squad were several non-college teams. One was called the East End Athletic Club, captained by John Lee, with club president George Goertz. The East Ends should not be confused with the famous East Ends of Fall River, Massachusetts. East Ends of Fall River was one of the first club soccer teams in America, established in 1880 and later disbanded in 1891. In the first organized club game in Louisiana history, the YMGC defeated the East Ends by a score of two to one. The game consisted of two thirty-minute halves.

Although YMGC defeated the East Ends in this match, the East Ends would soon turn the tables. In the city championship in February of 1896, the first championship for soccer held in Louisiana, the East Ends defeated YMGC. Led by Newsham, Smith, and Schuppert, the East Ends played "a brilliant game."

Every indication supports that this was a game that was played according to rules extremely similar to today's rules. There were corner kicks. Teams played with two fullbacks, three halfbacks, five forwards, and one in goal. Goals only counted if they went under the bar, not over, despite illustrations of goals above the bar in the paper, as in rugby. There was one referee, Mr. H. Weinecke, and two linesmen, Mr. Commagere and Mr. Brown. This was a modern soccer game played in New Orleans in 1895.

Was this a professional league? It cannot be known for certain, although there is a fairly good likelihood that some of the players were paid. This quasi-professionalism would cause problems in the league a decade later.

There was a large number of people out at the Young Men's athletic grounds yesterday, attracted by the football game between the Y. M. G. C. and East End teams and the fast bicycling by the crack riders now training on the cement track. A fine view was obtained from the grand stand of both features, and cheers went up, now for a fine burst of speed on the wheel and again for a fine football play.

Quite a number of Y. M. G. C. members were out to see their club team play their first game against another club. Both teams turned out as selected, and soon after 11 o'clock the captains tossed the coin for choice of ends and the teams lined up. Two halves of thirty minutes' play were agreed on.

Whitehouse won the toss and elected to play the first half with a slight wind. The East Ends kicked off from center, and the opening exchanges were in their favor, but very soon the ball was brought down the field by the Y. M. G. C. half-backs and the play was kept for a time in front of the East End goal. Several "corners" were gained by the attacking side, but no score was made from them, the East End full-backs and goal-keeper playing at that time very well. After Whitehouse had sent in two hot shots, one of which was cleverly stopped by the goal-keeper and the other just went over the bar instead of under, a combined rush of forwards resulted in the ball being put through by Bridges, about fifteen minutes from the start.

The play was then more even to the end of the first half, no more goals being scored. The weather was too warm for football and the players all seemed glad to take a ten minutes' rest. On lining up for the second half the East Ends played in a determined manner, and tried hard to equalize the score, which they did in about ten minutes. Then it was that the wearers of the black and old gold began, in turn, to play harder. The East End full-backs now inaugurated a defensive game and stayed close in goal, which made it useless for the opposing forwards to try long shots at goal; consequently they commenced a series of short passing combination plays, and finally, after a scrimmage right in the East End goal mouth, when the ball passed from one forward to another, at least four taking part in it, the ball was put through by Center Forward Whitehouse. That put the Y. M. G. C. team in the lead again, and that fact, together with the hard game, began to tell on the East Enders, and their play for the remaining eight minutes was not so good, though they were by no means done for, and gave the opposing full-backs several anxious times, but the latter were equal to the occasion. Every player on the field was glad to hear Referee H. Weinecke blow the whistle and call "Time." Final score: Two goals to one in favor of Y. M. G. C.

The game proved a very interesting one on account of its evenness and a large number of good plays.

For the winners, the two full-backs, Holmes and Tusson, played a very safe game, and kicked stronger than usual, particularly in the second half. Hurt, at center half, played a strong game from beginning to end. His wings, Geary and J. Prevost, often had a great amount of work to do, and did it well, till near the end, when they began to tire. The forwards all played well, Norris showing the most improved form.

For the losers, their captain, Lee, was exceedingly tricky at left wing forward, and made several long runs with the ball at his feet. In the second half he played at halfback, and did the bulk of the work there. The goal-keeper was very cool and made several brilliant saves.

Towards the end of the game the better condition of the winners prevented any further score against them. The same teams will meet again in the near future. The management of the Southern Wheelmen offered a cup for the same teams to play for at their bicycle meet next Saturday, but owing to the inability of the East End Club to raise a team on that day the offer had to be declined.

The teams lined up as follows:

Y. M. G. C.	Position.	East End.
T. Bradford	Goal	P. Goertz
Holmes	Right full-back	Croall
Tusson	Left full-back	Smith
J. Geary	Right half-back	Haug
L. S. Hurt	Center half-back	H. Maher
J. Prevost	Left half-back	Stamm
J. Lafaye	Right forward	Schubert
Norris	Right forward	Berlinger
Whitehouse (capt.)	Center forward	Nevette
S. Lafaye	Left forward	Lee (capt.)
Bridges	Left forward	Luelch

Referee—Mr. H. Weinecke. Linesmen—Mr. Commodore and Mr. Brown. Score: Y. M. G. C., goals 2; East Ends, goals 1.

The Daily Picayune, December 16, 1895.

The inaugural season of athletic club soccer lasted from November through March of 1896. The Eureka Rifle Club, the Rangers, the Harvester team, the Edgewater team, and the Southern Wheelmen, a cyclist club, joined the YMGC and East End Athletic Club in the league. Games were played at Sportsman's Park, Tulane's field, the Jackson Barracks Green and the Lesseps Street Green, located near the River just downriver from the French Quarter.

> **FOOTBALL.**
>
> **TWO GAMES ARRANGED FOR SUNDAY.**
>
> TO-MORROW there will be games of association football. The Y. M. G. C. will play the Rangers at the Fair grounds, and a mixed team of the Southern Wheelmen and Y. M. G. C. will contest with the East Ends at the bicycle track inclosure. Both games are scheduled for 11 a. m., and there will be no admission charged. L. S. Burt will captain the Y. M. G. C. team against the Rangers, and Prof. Whitehouse will lead the Y. M. G. C.-Wheelmen combination against the East Ends. The East Ends will play their strongest team, including the new men who have played with English clubs.
>
> Y. M. G. C. Team—Goal, T. Bradford; fullbacks, Holmes and Tusson; half-backs, J. Geary, Norris and J. Provost; forwards, Murphy, S. Lafayo, L. S. Burt, Bridges, N. Ehrlish.
>
> Ranger Team—Goal, A. Socha; full-backs, McCoy and Rober; half-backs, E. Socha, Donovan and Comfort; forwards, Tobin, Lambard, Graham, Hill and Brown.
>
> Referee—Mr. Commagere.

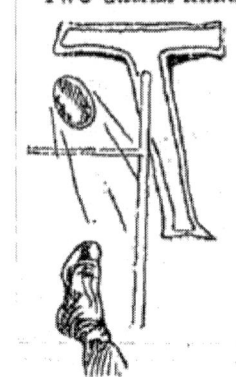

The Daily Picayune, January 25, 1896.

The New Orleans Association Football League of 1895-1896 had at least eleven member teams: seven clubs and four colleges. The popularity of soccer was not limited to young men. "Association football has even found its way among the youths below Canal street (sic), and on Sunday there was a very creditable game played between two of these boy-teams. One of the teams was known as the Telbly and the other team as the B. Thompsons. The score stood 1 to 0 in favor of the Telblys."

The league continued the following year. In one of the first games of the 1896-1897 season, the first drawing of true soccer and of a soccer player, Captain Carrere, appeared in a Louisiana paper. The YMGC's Prof. Whitehouse officiated the game, watched by a "good number of spectators" at Sportsman's Park. The Edgewaters defeated the East Ends 1-0. With the win, the Edgewaters took home two trophies, which had previously been handed out to the best team at the German Volksfest and the "letter carriers' festival." From that bit of information about the trophies, we can conclude that there was some overlap of this league with the festivals held by German and Irish civic organizations dating all the way back to 1858.

The Daily Picayune, October 19, 1896.

The roster for the East Ends shows a mostly Anglo-Saxon and German team, with surnames like Nelson, Newsham, Smith, Lee, Schubert and Goetz. The Edgewater roster reveals a German, Irish, and French squad. Names of the Edgewaters include Witzel, Carrere, O'Conner, O'Neil, DeBlanc, and Reuter.

Tulane's intervarsity squad continued its struggles in 1896. On November 14, the Greenies faced the University of Texas. The Longhorns came away with a resounding 12 to 4 victory, in a game held on the "Tulane athletic grounds, opposite Audubon park." Notably, 800 people watched the game. Although this game likely was a hybrid between soccer and football (and likely it was a lot closer to American football than soccer) the local papers reported it being an association football match. This confusion highlights that even amongst sports writers in the 1890s, there were less than distinct lines between sports. We do get an idea of what football-soccer uniforms consisted of at the time, thanks to an illustration of one the captains of the Texas squad.

The Daily Picayune, November 15, 1896.

The 1896-1897 season witnessed the addition of a couple of squads and the departure of others. One new team hailed from Jackson Barracks. These soldiers were from New York, had played the game before, and were managed by Corporal Quinn of Battery G (*The Daily Picayune,* November 16, 1896). The team took the name of "Haskins Football Club," named after Major Haskins of the command. The city soccer league claimed six clubs at this point: East Ends, Edgewaters, Eurekas, Enterprise of Algiers, and the Haskins (*The Daily Picayune,*

November 28, 1896). Games were scheduled from November through March.

While this was supposed to be an amateur league, admission was charged to some of the games. "Popular prices will be charged (and) there is sure to be a large number of spectators (*The Daily Picayune*, December 19, 1896)." Admission at Athletic Park was 25 cents for men, 15 cents for boys, and free for ladies. In today's money, tickets would have run about $7 and $4, respectively.

The move from Sportsman's Park to Athletic Park was a fairly major one in the development of the game. The previous season games were at Sportsman's Park and other open fields where admission was not charged.

Athletic Park was something different. It was a real field with enclosures and seats for the fans. Located on the southeast intersection of Tulane and Carrollton Avenues, Athletic Park was replaced by the White City Amusement Park. In 1915, Heinemann Park replaced White City. Heinemann Park was renamed in 1938 to its better-known name, Pelican Stadium. Pelican Stadium, of course, was the stadium for New Orleans' professional baseball team, the Pelicans. Today, all that remains as evidence of that location's history is a historical marker placed in front of a Burger King.

Association Football
TO-DAY,
At Athletic Park.
Two League Games,
AT 8 P. M. AND 4:10 P. M.
ADMISSION, 25c; boys 15c; ladies free.
The Daily Picayune, December 27, 1896.

Regularly officiating the matches were Professor Whitehouse from the YMGC, Mr. A. Carrere from the Edgewaters, D. Newsham from the East Ends, Mr. Gallagher and a Mr. E. J. Murphy. Most games were held on Sunday in Athletic Park, but some games were played at Ferran's Park in Carrollton and Jackson Barracks. The teams even played on Christmas day, in an exhibition that preceded a rugby game.

The championship of the 1896-1897 season was a grand match between the East Ends and Edgewater. The crowds surrounded the field at Jackson Barracks and saw a great game. East Ends struck first with a "combination playing and passing which was the prettiest seen in any game this season" (*Daily Picayune*, April 19, 1897). East Ends put another goal in the net to finish the game as 2-0 winners. It was the East Ends' second city championship in a row.

The following was the starting roster for the East Ends. Roach (goal); Dan Newsham and A.N. O'Neil (fullbacks); Blum, Nelson, and Smith (halfbacks); Lee, Lucich, Maher, Hamilton, and Goertz (forwards).

The Crescents formed during the summer of 1897 and joined the New Orleans Association Football League. The team was captained by Steve Pier, a Scotsman, and managed by George Hang. Based on the address of the players, this time most likely formed in what today is called Bywater in New Orleans.

The league of 1897-1898, again playing from November to April, consisted of seven teams: East Ends, Edgewaters, YMGC, the Crescents, and few other newcomers to the game: the Silver Leaves (captained by L.

Slilans) and the Fred Sluggers (captained by F. Powell). Of note during this season, a benefit game was held to help A. Nivette, who had lost his leg in a railroad accident during the summer. "Nivette was one of the good players of the city, and all his old friends thought a benefit game would be a small appreciation of their sincere friendship (*The Daily Picayune*, December 12, 1897)."

Most of the non-athletic club members of this league were blue-collar workers, evidenced by the man who lost his leg on the railroad. The athletic club teams, on the other hand, were affluent and the most affluent of the athletic clubs was the YMGC. Most of their matches during '97-'98 were held at Athletic Park, which cost a good bit of money to rent. The rest of the teams had less luxurious accommodations for their games, with matches played in Jackson Barracks and on the levee between Montegut and Clouet Streets.

The 1897-1898 season was important for two other reasons. First, the league took on an official name: The New Orleans Association Football League. Second, in January of that season, the teams gathered to create an all-star team (*The Daily Picayune*, January 12, 1898). This team traveled to St. Louis and Cincinnati to play the best of those city's teams, which included the best teams in America. Sadly, there is no record of how the New Orleans team fared against these Midwestern squads. The fact that the team traveled such a great distance, though, showed how important the game was to the players.

Soccer was popular amongst several clubs in New Orleans at the turn of the century. How did the general public feel about the game? Did children play the game in the streets? One good indication that it was growing in popularity outside the athletic club scene comes from a paper advertisement of The H. & D. Folsom Arms Co., 115 Decatur Street. In this add, for the first time in Louisiana, we know that soccer balls were for sale in a store.

Crescent Air Rifle—Barrel made of steel, price **$1.00**.
Association Football, 50c, 60c, 75c.
Rugby Footballs—(leather) for boys, **$1.00**.
Rugby Match Footballs—Made of best tanned hide leather, **$2.00**.

The Daily Picayune, December 18, 1898.

Nationally, several professional leagues attempted to form in the 1890s. Examples include the American Amateur Football Association, the American League of Professional Football, the National Association Foot Ball League, and in 1901, the Association Football League. The AFL awarded franchises to St. Louis, Chicago, Milwaukee, and Detroit. Soccer in the Midwest flourished. Meanwhile, in New Orleans, soccer floundered in the late 1890s.

After several successful seasons (1895-1898), the New Orleans Association Football League dropped off the media's radar until 1905. If it existed, the records cannot be found. When the league returned, a major battle would ensue over the issue of professionalizing the league or remaining an amateur league.

1905-1907:
The Rebirth of the New Orleans Association Football League

Soccer proponents in Louisiana hibernated in the earliest years of the twentieth century. In a few pockets in the Midwest and the Northeast, soccer flourished, but it was lagging far behind football and baseball. In 1905, American football had reached a crossroads, a moment that would either make or break the sport. It was a national moment that would make or break soccer as well.

Earlier in that year, nearly twenty American football players were killed in separate on-field accidents. The game was increasingly violent, as matches would turn into fistfights and few players wore any padding for the rough and tumble collisions.

Sports writers opined that the sport of football was an "old-fashioned form of manslaughter." Much like the current frenzy seeking to reduce concussions in football, advocates for the cause sought allies in the medical field, in the media, and in politics. The national uproar reached a fever pitch when college presidents met with President Theodore Roosevelt.

The college presidents' goal was to persuade the President to ban football from college campuses. This would, in essence, kill the sport of football because the game was nurtured and thrived in college more than anywhere else.

This period presented American soccer with one of its greatest opportunities to garner national interest and a following. By 1906, soccer was in a prime position to succeed to the throne of American sports.

Soccer was already the official sport of England, with whom America had very close political, economic, and social ties. There were large soccer fanbases in New England and Canada. Promoters of the sport staged several international tours, bringing teams from the Pilgrim Association in England to play professional teams in America. In the picture below, the Thistles of New York faced one such team in front of thousands at the New York Polo Grounds.

The Pilgrim Association not only played matches. They also visited with Harvard President Charles Eliot, the leader in the campaign to eliminate football from his school. The captain of the English soccer club, Fred Milnes, sought Eliot's cooperation in making soccer a universal game in the American colleges.

As a sign of his intent, Milnes offered a silver trophy, valued at $825, to give to the first winners. Milnes petitioned members of the New York Athletic Club and the Crescent Athletic Club in New York as well (*The Daily Picayune*, October 17, 1905). Soccer was on the verge.

The media was behind soccer as well. The New Orleans sports writer George Sands wrote, "Outside of boxing and the present day form of football, "socker" is the toughest sort of a field game known to Anglo-Saxons." Sands concluded incorrectly "there has never been a game played in New Orleans." Newspaper archives clearly indicate, as we have already seen, that soccer was played in New Orleans in 1858. Incorrect superlative language in regards to soccer firsts long plagued Louisiana. Even into the 1990s, press members wrote about "firsts," that were not firsts at all.

The New Orleans Item, January 28, 1906

Roosevelt, however, loved football and he did not want to see the sport abolished. The President insisted on a compromise with the college presidents. The college presidents agreed to keep the sport at their schools so long as the rules changed. Some of those rules included the introduction of the forward pass, the prohibition against mass formations, and the change from a 5 yard first down to a 10 yard first down.

The rule changes in football saved the sport. Indeed, more than save the sport, the rule changes helped propel the sport. Although football would not surpass baseball as America's favorite sport until 1972, football did see a fairly steady climb in all those years leading up to 1972 (Carroll, Joseph. "Football Reaches Historic Popularity Levels in Gallup Poll." Gallup, 19 Jan. 2007).

In 1905, the new football rules book written by Walter Camp appeared for sale in *The New Orleans Item*. Right below it was an advertisement for the *Association Football Guide* by Jerome Flannery.

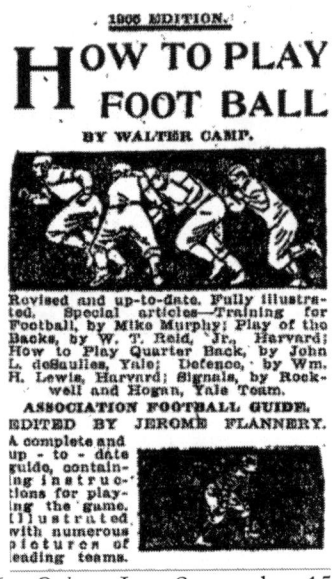

The New Orleans Item, September 15, 1905.

Football saved itself; there was no sporting void that soccer could fill. That opening soccer might have used to assert itself as an American sport closed. Indeed, soccer fell further behind football on the national stage as a result of football's ability to rally behind the new rules.

In Louisiana, however, soccer was growing. A positive sign was found on the field at the Holy Cross College campus on November the 18th, 1905. There, the Holy Cross College boys defeated the players from Sacred Heart School by a score of 1-0. This may have been the first high school soccer game in Louisiana, if these were in fact high schools. The term college in the early 20th century has a nebulous meaning, so it is possible that these two teams were what today would be high schools.

SOCKER FOOTBALL.

Holy Cross College Defeats the Students of Sacred Heart School.

Yesterday on the Holy Cross College Campus a large crowd witnessed a splendid game of socker football between the College Juniors and the sturdy boys of Sacred Heart School. A close game was expected, as both teams were thoroughly trained in the fine points of the play, and evenly matched in size and age. The visitors started off with a rush and soon threatened the College Boys' goal. Excellent defense work, however, kept the ball from passing between the goal posts. Both teams soon settled down to real scientific work and back and forth across the field the ball flew. When time was called for the first half, the score stood: Holy Cross, 0; Sacred Heart, 0. On the resumption of play the College Boys started with a vim which augured victory. The visitors, however were equal to the occasion and every attempt to secure a goal was denied. It was not till toward the close of the second half, that Boos, in a free kick from the eighteen yard line, booted the ball squarely between the goal posts, to the great joy of the college rooters. The visitors struggled desperately to tie the score, but their efforts were without succes. When time was called the score stood: Holy Cross, one goal; Sacred Heart nil. For the Sacred Heart School the playing of Martin, Maguire, LaHare, Dosset, and Schiffler won the applause of the spectators; while Commander, Ciental, Holzenthal, Boos, and LaCroix, played brilliantly for the college boys.

Those who witnessed the first game of Socker or Association football ever played in New Orleans by college students, were much pleased at the entire absence of roughness and injuries which are such a conspicuous feature of Rugby. Another match between the same teams will be played next week in the City Park.

The Daily Picayune, November 19, 1905.

The New Orleans Association Football League, absent for nearly a decade, recommenced in the Spring of 1906. During the interlude, teams likely continued to play in the streets, on open greens, and on the levee of New Orleans. Nonetheless, any soccer played was sporadic, probably unorganized, and certainly unpublicized.

According to *New Orleans Item* sports editor, Will R. Hamilton, the 1906 Spring season did not see much participation. By the Autumn, Hamilton wrote, "There is great interest being taken in the latest attempt of several of the sporting men of the city in making a mighty try to revive the English association game of football, or, as it is better known, socker" (*The New Orleans Item*, September 22, 1907).

Wanting to grow soccer, James Carrigan chaired a meeting in September of 1907. At the meeting, members of four groups: O'Hare-Carrigan, YMGC, Young Men's Christian Association (YMCA) and Young Men's Hebrew Association (YMHA) agreed to participate. Games were to be held at newly renovated Sportsman's Park.

As the fall season got underway, the leader of the pack was the Young Men's Gymnastic Club. The club, if you recall, had made a trip to St. Louis in 1898 to play several clubs there. In November of 1906, they wanted a St. Louis squad to return the favor. The YMGC sent an invitation, or rather, a challenge to Finnegan's West End of St. Louis, one of the top teams in the nation. The match was to be held on Thanksgiving Day, 1906. Rumors circulated that West End accepted the invitation. However, there is no record of the game ever having been played (*The New Orleans Item*, November 3, 1906).

The league's first publicized match in a decade was a game between YMGC and O'Hare-Carrigan played on January 27, 1907. O'Hare-Carrigan was a team sponsored by its namesake, a sporting goods store owned by one of the team members and local soccer organizer, James Carrigan. The store was located in what is today the Warehouse District of New Orleans, then an Irish American area of town. The team was made up of neighborhood men, mostly Irish, but there was at least one Hispanic team member, Mr. Gonzalez.

FAST "SOCKER" FOOTBALL WILL BE ON TO-MORROW

If you wish to see a cracking game of association football go to Sportsmen's Park about 10:30 to-morrow morning and see the O'Hare-Carrigan eleven go up against the aggregation from the Y. M. G. C. It will be a championship league contest and a hummer from start to finish, as the teams are very evenly matched.

To-Morrow's Line Up.

The line-up will be as follows: Y. M. G. C.—Stewart, goal; Hoffman, W. McLachlin, fullbacks; Levy, A. McLachlin, Gillittle, halfbacks; Blumphin, Noxie, right wings; Grant, McClay, left wings; Balmer, center forward.

O'Hare-Carrigans—Smith, goal; Carrigan, Brandon, fullbacks; Sanders, Le Blanc, Roach, halfbacks; Hickey, Butcher, right wings; Lucich, Gonzales, left wings; Cuss, center forward.

The New Orleans Item, January 26, 1907.

The league of 1907 grew and became better organized. The Starlights, a team consisting mostly of members from what today would be the Holy Cross, Bywater and Marigny neighborhoods, joined. Some of the first members of the Starlights had the surnames Superein, Hoffman, Haiderloin, Florian, Butcher, Thebucq, Morgan, Donald, Colman, and Asola (*N.O. Item*, October 5, 1907). James Carrigan's stature in the league appears to have been great, as a player, as an organizer, and as a referee.

Games were being held weekly on Sundays in Sportsman's Park. Most matches were evenly played, with 1-0 and 1-1 scores regularly reported. By October of 1907, the leaders of the league had big plans.

To signify these changing times, the league decided to change its name from the New Orleans Association Football League to the New Orleans Soccer League, a name that would only last a few months.

Charter members of this newly named league included the YMGC, the YMHA, the Catholic Ushers, the Starlights, O'Hare-Carrigan, and Phelps Tulane. In addition to these six squads, the league sought membership from the Southern Athletic Club (SAC) and the Phoenix Athletic Club, a popular downtown gym located on 3037 North Rampart in the Wiltz Gym. The SAC fielded a team briefly, but none of their games were recorded.

The league members looked for teams outside New Orleans as well. A team from Shreveport made the trip to New Orleans to play. This marks the first time soccer in north Louisiana was recorded since the Confederate soldiers from north Louisiana played a game in Arkansas in 1861. The port city of Mobile, Alabama also fielded a team that season. While much has been written on the history of soccer on the East Coast and in the Midwest during this page, no attention has yet been given to soccer on the Gulf Coast at the beginning of the twentieth century.

Oddly enough, the East End Football Association existed, but was not invited to join the league. As a result, the manager of the East Ends, a Mr. Roth, advertised in the paper and sought "any soccer team in or out of the city" (*N.O. Item*, 10/25/1907). There is no record of him finding any takers.

The biggest move the league made, however, was a plan to rent the local baseball park to play in during the winter of 1907-1908. "After the league is organized the teams can play on a regular schedule and after the support of the public is assured the league can bring down soccer teams of national reputation from St. Louis, Chicago, and other cities."

This league certainly did not lack in aspirations. Its leaders were elected at this meeting of great expectations. The President was Professor O. B. Schoenfeld of the YMHA, Vice President was Mr. Balmer of the

YMGC, and also of the YMGC was Mr. Stewart, who was chosen to be both Secretary and Treasurer of the league.

The league's leaders met with Secretary Heinemann of the Pelican baseball team. As smoke wafted in the air, the gentlemen, robed in suits bought in the finest clothiers on Canal Street, agreed that baseball and soccer could have a future together in New Orleans. At stake was the grand notion that the two sports could be symbiotic.

Sunday baseball games, they agreed, would be paired with soccer matches. The baseball team would benefit from the soccer fans showing at the games. The soccer league would benefit from publicity and baseball fans.

For a while, it looked like it would work. Headlines in all the papers in New Orleans drew attention to the league and to individuals in the league. Interest was stirred with the publication of the first photograph of a soccer player in a Louisiana paper (below).

The chosen man was Mr. Stewart, a member of the YMGC team. "He is perhaps the most expert player in New Orleans," wrote one writer. His resume certainly backed up that claim. Swift, sure-handed, rangy, Stewart had been star goalkeeper for the Baltimore team that won the East Coast league in 1894, defeating the top teams in Philadelphia, Washingston, Boston, Brooklyn, and New York. He also played the same position for the All-American squad which defeated the All-Canadian squad in 1892, which represented some of the first international soccer games in the world.

STAR SOCCER PLAYER.

The New Orleans Item, October 17, 1907.

Exhibition for Sunday.

It is planned by the two teams, the O'Hare-Carrigans and the Y. M. G. C., to secure a big baseball park in which to play during this winter. After the league is organized the teams can play on a regular schedule and after the support of the public is assured the league can bring down soccer teams of national reputation from St. Louis, Chicago and other cities.

There has been some talk of giving an exhibition of soccer at Athletic Park next Sunday. The O.-Cs. and the Y. M. G. Cs. have already played two splendid games, one of which was a tie, and these clubs are well prepared to give a scientific exhibition.

It is said the Phelps-Tulanes are also organizing a soccer team.

The New Orleans Item, October 15, 1907.

The buildup for the first baseball-soccer doubleheader was great. The game was "soon to be introduced to this city on an extensive scale" (*N.O. Item*, 10/17/1907). *The New Orleans Item* was daily doing its best to draw spectators' interest. The sports editor published in the week leading up to the game several syndicated articles like the one below, which described the general history of soccer and the history of soccer in the United States.

SOCCER SPREADS ALL OVER COUNTRY

BY SIR ERNEST CECIL COCHRANE.

Association football, as a winter recreation, does not claim any ancient lineage. Records of football are found as far back as 1583, but it was a rough and tumble contest in those days, and had nothing in form or style with that which has been popularized since the modern revival, which is dated from 1859-69, when, from the primitive commencement of a mere kickabout, sprang a number of clubs, the progenitor of the present world-wide organizations of Association football. The Pilgrim Fathers of football had to depend upon the wild excitement of practice games in default of the stern joy which members of an organization feel in meeting worthy rivals on the playing field, and despite many oppositions and objections it now holds the premier position among winter sports.

For many years the Rugby game was the preponderating or the only code of football in evidence, but the development of the Association game gradually spread as its advantages became more and more apparent. There was for a long time a wide divergence of playing rules, but the unification of the various systems of play steadily enlarged the area and at the same time extended the influence of the game.

The keen rivalry, often amounting to fierceness, and frequently resulting in serious accidents, rendered it necessary to adopt a more refined and less brutal style of game. The curtailment of individual play and the development to the highest the united powers of an eleven, as well as tending to bring out the latent powers of every member in equal ratio, was the primary object of those responsible for the introduction of Association football. The well being of a side depends upon the way in which every member is utilized. A maximum of proficiency with a minimum of expenditure of force—that is, of individual force—are the principles upon which Association football is constructed.

How Game Started Here.

The development of association football in the United States has been in gradual progress for more than two decades. New York and Philadelphia led the way, quickly followed by Fall River, Trenton and Paterson, in the East, and Detroit and Chicago in the West. Many clubs were organized, but the sport-loving public did not see the game under its most favorable conditions. An effort was made to introduce it into the varsities and colleges, but the effort met with little success. Such a radical change was not likely to be made without a good deal of diversity of opinion and opposition. It was some time before the college football mind became attuned to the suggestion of the change, but after a spirited resistance the opposition broke down and tacitly admitted that the game had its advantages. With the first wedge entered the crevice, was gradually pried open, and a league of clubs from the leading collegiate institutions followed and is now thriving.

On the day of the big game between YMGC and O'Hare-Carrigan, the league Vice President and member of the YMGC, Mr. Balmer, made the front and center of *The New Orleans Item* sports section. He appears to be wearing a uniform consisting of shin guards, long pants, and a sweater with a strip across the chest. The paper described him as "instrumental in organizing the local league. He is considered a star at the game will be seen in action at Athletic Park this afternoon."

The New Orleans Item, October 20, 1907.

Optimistically, organizers expected a few thousand attendees. When New Orleanians opened the paper on Monday morning, however, there was no write-up of the game. The next mention of soccer in the papers is on Thursday, when it was announced that Tad Gormley, the newly arrived native of Boston, would help with the YMGC soccer team.

Gormley was a well-respected athletic trainer that became one of the major figures in New Orleans athletics during the next century. The stadium in City Park where high school soccer championships are held is named after him.

DIRECTOR GORMLEY.

The New Orleans Item, October 24, 1907.

Will R. Hamilton's efforts to get the public out to the soccer games on Sundays before the Pelican baseball games were ultimately a failure. In an October 28, 1907, Hamilton wrote an editorial extolling the virtues of soccer over football: it is played well in the winter and spectators have a perfect view of what's happening from far away. All that mattered not. The people of New Orleans did not find soccer interesting.

It did not seem like the most likely or the most fruitful time a professional league would form in New Orleans. In November of 1907, however, that was exactly what happened.

1907-1908:
The Amateur and Professional Split

In 1907, soccer had a bright future in certain regions of America. Successful amateur leagues existed in cities like New York, St. Louis, Pittsburgh, Cleveland, Chicago, Philadelphia, Baltimore, and even on the West Coast in San Francisco and Tacoma. The first broad governing body, the American Football Association (AFA), gained traction and its rules were the American standard. The American Cup, sponsored by the AFA, the first national soccer tournament in America, grew in significance as more teams entered.

Across the country, West Hudson Athletic Club (WHAC), a team of Scottish American amateurs in New Jersey, was the emerging force in inter-league play in the Northeast. After winning the American Cup, the team had a big decision to make: stay in their local amateur league or join the newly reconstituted, National Association Football League. West Hudson chose to join the professional league, a league that eventually formed the American Soccer League (1923-1990).

In New Orleans a similar scenario unfolded. The healthy amateur New Orleans Association Football League attracted some of the best soccer players in America. Much of this talent came to play not because soccer afforded them a healthy salary. They came because the trade industry in New Orleans boomed.

At the turn of the century, New Orleans was one of the busiest ports in the world. The city still dealt with a profitable, though dwindling, cotton trade. Much of the cotton was destined for the cotton mills of England and Scotland.

A burgeoning trade was the fruit trade. The Vaccaro brothers and Samuel Zemurray separately began their New Orleans-based banana businesses that strengthened the connection between New Orleans and Central America. The J. Aron Company of New Orleans also linked the city to Central and South America through a rapidly growing coffee trade. New Orleans was an international port and its new residents brought with them their own language, religion, food, and games.

Formally established in 1904, FIFA's founding marked the beginning of the explosion of organized international soccer. Even before its founding, though, soccer was very popular in most of Western Europe, and Western Europe's reach was great. Imperial colonialism stretched its tentacles throughout the world. Colonialism was not limited to economic exploitation of foreign lands. In addition to taking from these lands, Western European nations left something as well: their culture. Whether or not these countries wanted that is a different topic. Nonetheless, it happened, and part of that culture was soccer.

As a result, soccer became wildly popular in places ranging from British Honduras to Hong Kong. The Scottish, almost a colony of the English themselves, were amongst the first exporters of the game. After the German and Irish immigrant communities looked to American football instead of soccer in the early 1880s, Scottish immigrants in Louisiana helped reintroduce the game in the late 1880s. The Scots did the same in Brazil in 1894 when Charles William Miller introduced the game there.

The Scottish contribution to the Louisiana game in the late 1800s and later cannot be overstated. It was not just Louisiana, though. Throughout America, the Scottish influence greatly impacted the success and style of the game.

"The influence of Scots and Scotland in the development of soccer is paramount...throughout the British colonial possessions and other countries where British commercial and industrial expertise was established. The 'Scotch professors' changed the nature of soccer by adopting the passing game instead of the dribbling game. Prior to this development, the strategy had been to get behind the man with the ball and rush forward in a mighty mass, with the hope of forcing the ball through the goal. The Scots decided that the ball could travel faster and more efficiently than a man, so they kept more players in defense, spread their forwards to include two wingers, and learned to pass accurately to fellow players rather than rely on the almighty kick and the rush to catch up with the ball" (Bill Murray, *The World's Game: A History of Soccer*).

This international growth and development of soccer was important to the later history of soccer in Louisiana, as former British colonies, notably those in Latin America, exported the game to America. The Latin infusion in the early 1900s was paramount in the establishment of soccer organizations that exist even to this day. The early soccer roots of Louisiana did not have the same continuous impact, lasting to the present, which is one reason so little is known about the early history. At the turn of the century, though, most soccer players in New Orleans were Irish, Scottish, English, and from the East Coast of the United States.

In 1907, some of the teams in the New Orleans Football Association League attracted players by offering unknown amounts of money. In other words, technically, the league had become professional, or at least, semi-professional. Most players in the league played for the sport, but some were paid.

The pay-for-play aspect disturbed members of the Young Men's Gymnastic Club. The YMGC was a member of the Amateur Athletic Union (AAU), and as a member, it was required to be an amateurs-only club. If the New Orleans Association Football League became a professional league, the YMGC would lose its amateur status. While that prospect may not have bothered YMGC soccer players, it mattered to the club as a whole.

The YMGC was not willing to sacrifice its amateur status. The club wanted its members in other sports, like running, swimming, and tennis, to be allowed to compete in AAU events. Surrendering its amateur status for soccer was not a sacrifice the club was willing to make.

On the other side of the issue were members of the New Orleans Association Football League that wanted the sport to progress and improve. They saw professionalizing the league as the only way to assure that those goals were achieved. They also knew that the league had some of the best soccer players in America, and perhaps, the world.

Said James Carrigan, leader of the O'Hare-Carrigan squad and league spokesman:

> "It is the aim of the League to give the public the best there is in association football. They could not be hampered with a lot of petty rulings of the A.A.U., as the League's teams are largely composed of men who have filled positions in the best professional teams in the United States and abroad. It would be an imposition on the public to invite them to Athletic Park to see a lot of green men attempting to play the game when we have in our midst men who have made a life study of it and are thorough masters of the game" (*The New Orleans Item*, November 14, 1907).

Ultimately, the league split. This split had enormous ramifications to the future of the sport. The YMGC remained part of the amateur league in New Orleans. The club also was the leader in that league and worked with the Young Men's Hebrew Association to shore up the amateur adult game in the city.

The professionals were able to cobble together a four-team league. They included the Starlights, Phelps-Tulane, O'Hare-Carrigan, and St. Andrews. St. Andrews was an amalgamation of players from the YMGC and the YMHA who wanted to see professional soccer in New Orleans to succeed. The manager of St. Andrews, A.W. Steward, the former star for the Baltimore and All-American team, anchored the team. The rosters for the four teams were as follows.

Phelps-Tulane: Middleton (goal); Gillespie and Keedle (backs); Gibbs, Gilbert, and Hill (halfbacks); Ferine and Chance (right wing); Target (center); Moir and Henry (left wing).

Starlights: Albert (goal); Thiery and Moinet (backs); Hunterline, Arsola, and Hoffman (halfbacks); Trailueo and Florande (right wing); Donald (center); Ruther and Earhart (left wing).

St. Andrews: Stewart (goal); William McLachlan and Hoffman (backs); Cordon and Blamphin and Vallor (halfbacks); McClay and A. McLachlan (right wing); Grant (center); Fenwick and Balmer (left wing).

O'Hare-Carrigans: Good (goal); and Carrigan (backs); Doddridge, Aitken, and Elliot (halfbacks); Burnham and Frances (right wing); Fairweather (center); Yonker and Arbroth (left wing).

The league leased Athletic Park for three months, from November to February of 1908. New Orleans media response to the league was less than enthusiastic. *The Daily Picayune,* whose editors were part of the same social circles as members of the YMGC, lost interest in soccer once the elitist YMGC left the league. The loss of the YMGC was enormous. The YMGC's participation in soccer gave the sport legitimacy in the eyes affluent in Louisiana and the South. With the club no longer involved in top-flight soccer, the sport fell to the fringes of culture. But what if the league had not split and the YMGC had remained? Although it is counterfactual history, had the YMGC not withdrawn, soccer might have become an intimate part of New Orleans culture during the early 1900s. New Orleans, as a result, might have become one of the capitals of American soccer. Of all the papers, the only paper that noticed the league was the afternoon publication, *The New Orleans Item.*

Public response at the park was tepid as well. The limited backing by the media and the withdrawal of the YMGC doomed the professional league from the get-go. Soccer failed to capture the New Orleans mind and the largest crowd any of the teams drew was described as "fair." The agreement that the amateur league had with the baseball Pelicans to play back-to-back games in order to benefit both baseball and soccer did not extend beyond the first year. The league struggled to stay afloat.

The soccer scene was not all terrible, however. St. Andrews hosted a Cotton Exchange team that was filled with members from the Liverpool Ramblers. This match on Thanksgiving Day of 1907 was the first international soccer match held in New Orleans.

COTTON MEN PLAY SOCCER

The Cotton Exchange soccer football team on Thanksgiving Day will play the St. Andrew team at Athletic Park. This game promises to be very interesting, from the fact that a good many of the players on the Cotton Exchange team were members of the Liverpool Ramblers, a team of the famous cotton men of Liverpool.

Captain H. Vick, who has played soccer football for a number of years in the old country, believes he can show the locals a thing or two about the game. Captain Stewart, of the St. Andrew team, thinks his team will be able to convince the exchange team they don't know so much about it after all.

The New Orleans Item, November 26, 1907.

The front-runners of the league were O'Hare-Carrigan and Phelps-Tulane. This rivalry produced a large $100 (about $2500 today) wager between the two teams that was settled on the field. In a hard fought battle with "both teams playing for blood" the O'Hare-Carrigan team won 3-1, including two goals scored by John Fairweather, pictured below with an O'Hare jersey. Phelps-Tulane's only goal was an own goal.

The New Orleans Item, November 30, 1907.

Phelps-Tulane avenged that loss in January of 1908. The Oharrigans, as they were sometimes called, fell to Phelps-Tulane 1-4. One spectator said after the game, "I actually believe that Phelps-Tulane could beat any bunch of soccer players in this country if they played together like that for another year" (*The New Orleans Item*, January 13, 1908). That boisterous, confident claim – a soccer team from 1908 New Orleans being the best soccer team in America --was not as far-fetched as it may sound today.

On that Phelps-Tulane roster were five Englishmen, five Scots, and a Welshman. It wasn't their nationalities that made them great. It was their skill, and they had proved their skill on some of the best soccer teams in the world at the time. Gillespie and Henry played for the Heart of Midlothian Football Club (Hearts), regularly amongst the top three teams in the Scottish League First Division during this period. Moir and Ferine played at Dundee United, also of the Scottish First Division, which might have been the best professional league in the world in those days. Keedle, Gilbert, and Hill played professionally in England. Middleton also played professionally in England and on one of the best squads in St. Louis. Phelps-Tulane possibly had the greatest collections of talent of any soccer team in Louisiana history.

It is unknown the origin of the name Phelps-Tulane. There is no indication that the team was sponsored by Tulane University. No player on the team was named Phelps. However, the Phelps family was a prominent one in New Orleans at this time. Ashton Phelps was a managing director of the *Picayune* after the Civil War and was on the Tulane Board of Administrators in 1907. His son, Esmond, was a basketball player at Tulane during that time. Perhaps the elder Phelps sponsored the team. If that is so, it is peculiar that the *N.O. Item*, not the *Picayune*, covered the team and league.

The Phelps-Tulane Association Football Team.
The New Orleans Item, December 4, 1907.

He Is the Leader of the Phelps-
Tulanes, One of the City's
Fastest Soccer Teams.
The New Orleans Item, December 2, 1907 (Capt. Henry pictured).

Ultimately, 1908 Phelps-Tulane would never get the chance to prove how it ranked against the rest of America's soccer teams. The match against O'Hare-Carrigan was the last professional soccer league game held in New Orleans for 85 years. The next professional team that appeared was the New Orleans Riverboat Gamblers in 1993. The final league standings were:

Phelps-Tulane	3-1
O'Hare-Carrigan	3-1
St. Andrews	1-2
Starlights	0-3

If one measures success of the league by its continuation, the league was a resounding failure. If the league's success is measured by the future of individual players, it was a success. Several players, as a result of their time in the New Orleans league, signed professional contracts in Europe. John Fairweather of O'Hare-Carrigan signed with Dundee United in Scotland. Mr. McDonald, also of O'Hare-Carrigan, signed with Clyde in the Spring of 1908. Interestingly, Dundee defeated Clyde to win the Scottish Cup in 1910. The match was replayed three times because of ties. More than 100,000 watched those games at Ibrox Park in Glasgow.

Other European squads raided the talent pool from which the professional league in New Orleans drew. Several on the Phelps-Tulane squad returned to the professional game in Britain as well. The league could not overcome the loss of talent and folded. A year later, James Carrigan tried to restart the league, but was unsuccessful.

Scotchmen Want to Start Another Soccer League Here

A soccer football league has been proposed for New Orleans. To this end several persons are trying to organize a couple of teams. J. J. Carrigan, of the O'Hare-Carrigan Sporting Company, has done the most toward the organizing of a league, and while he does not believe a full league of four teams can be formed here, he is of the opinion that two good teams might be organized to play a game for the benefit of some charity, preferably the doll and toy fund.

Mr. Carrigan has expressed his willingness of calling a meeting of soccer enthusiasts for the purpose of getting together several teams. He will probably make an announcement some time next week.

Soccer football is considered by many to be the equal if not superior to the college style of play. It is by far the most spectacular game and to the spectator it is very exciting. This game is played in England, Scotland and Ireland just as baseball is played here during the summer season, it being their national game.

While the local league of last season was not a profound success, there were a lot of things to contend with. The weather, for one thing, was against the teams, and then it was a new game in this part of the country.

Several of the men who played on the teams which composed last season's league have returned to the old country, and are now members of large teams. McDonald, who played full back with the O'Harrigans last season, is now a member of the Clyde team in Scotland. John Fairbrother is a member of the Dundee team. He played on one of the teams here last season.

The New Orleans Item, December 13, 1908.

With the pro game folded and the amateur league in shambles after the split, soccer again disappeared from the headlines. For all practical purposes, soccer amongst the Anglo-Saxon community in New Orleans, which by this point lived downtown and uptown, ceased to exist. Soccer's appeal to this social group — mostly wealthy and nativist -- did not regain a foothold until the 1970s, when playground recreational leagues and high school soccer began.

1909-1918:

American Football's Triumph Over Soccer

New Orleans rejected soccer after the professional New Orleans Football Association League folded. Clubs may have continued playing a sporadic game during these years, but it was just that, sporadic. When it was played, it was played for fun and exercise only. There was no effort made to bring teams together and form a league. In 1911, the YMGC played its last game in a "rare game" amongst YMGC members, captained by Mr. Blamphin. The author of the article wrote, "Soccer football will probably never become as popular in this country as regulation college football" (*The Daily Picayune,* November 4, 1911).

Regulation college football captured the minds and hearts of Louisiana. LSU and Tulane were soon to build their massive stadiums, which held tens of thousands of fans. Soccer was again an afterthought.

LSU's George Ellwood "Doc" Fenton serves a microcosm for the era. Fenton, a Pennsylvania native, was a tremendous athlete even as a boy. He was recruited to play soccer by St. Michael's College School, a Roman Catholic school in Toronto. There he became a master of the game and was a star in rugby as well. He was good enough to play soccer professionally in Europe. His life took a different track, though. Steered away from soccer because of a declining national interest in the sport, he looked to football.

Recruited by LSU, Fenton moved to Baton Rouge, where he became a sensation on the football field. Fenton played out his career on the LSU football field. It is unlikely he kicked a soccer ball again. Fenton and Louisiana chose football.

Did Tulane have a team at this point? It is uncertain. A weak argument could be made that Phelps-Tulane was a Tulane soccer team.

What is certain is that in 1912, the Louisiana Industrial Institute, which would become Louisiana Tech, started a "soccer football" program under Coach P.S. Prince.

> **FOOTBALL.**
>
> **SOCCOR FOOTBALL INTRODUCED.**
> RUSTON, LA., Dec. 14.—Coach P. S. Prince has introduced soccer football into the athletics of the Louisiana Industrial Institute. So far as is known this also marks the introduction of the game into Louisiana.
>
> *The Daily Picayune*, December 16, 1912.

Little else can be said about soccer in Louisiana during the 1910s. The sport may have caught on moderately in north and central Louisiana. The next mention of the game is on December 3, 1917, when, according to a *Times Picayune* article, soldiers at Camp Beauregard in Pineville were found playing football and soccer.

At the same time, the American Professional Football Conference (APFC), forerunner to the NFL, was organizing. Soon after, the APFC enjoyed the same popularity as college football. Soccer fell further behind and drifted apart from American culture.

1919-1922:
Dock Soccer Origins

The world became a much smaller place in 1919. After 16 million people died, World War I mercifully came to a close. Nations had built large navies. People from many countries had seen places they never had heard of before the war. International travel opened to an entirely different class of people. The Great War profoundly altered the way the countries interacted with others.

One way in which that was felt in New Orleans was the vast increase in foreign ships making portage in New Orleans. Before the war, most ships docking in New Orleans were domestic ships that either traded within the States or set sail abroad. After the war, there was a dramatic increase in foreign ships doing business in the Crescent City.

Soccer in Louisiana was dead at the end of the War. The native Louisianians who might have been interested in starting soccer leagues were either consumed by baseball and football or were disillusioned by the past failure of soccer to take hold in the state. The state needed new blood, rejuvenation from outsiders.

This period of globalization would do just that. The bourgeoning foreign trade, consisting mostly of bananas, coffee, and oil, brought also to Louisiana people who came from soccer loving lands. Soccer in Louisiana was stranded in a harsh desert, but in these global sailors and immigrants from Central America, Louisiana soccer would find a lush oasis in which to grow.

Dock soccer is a term that first appeared on the LAprepSoccer message boards around 2000. Members of the forum have since used the term jokingly to refer to competitive, machismo competitions of soccer between rivals. Dock soccer, however, perfectly describes a long period in

Louisiana soccer history, nearly a century long, or perhaps even longer. It was a period when, for large stretches, the only brand of soccer in the state was practiced and played by teams of sailors from the crews of visiting ships at the New Orleans ports.

Dock soccer apparently started before 1919. According to *The States Item* "there have been 'pick-up' team games by the crews of ships in port long before this [October 20, 1919] in New Orleans."

Dock soccer also was not confined to New Orleans. Games were played in Gulf Coast port towns like Pensacola and Galveston. The East Coast of America also saw a healthy dock soccer league. Indeed, one of the ways soccer became a global sport was through dock soccer. Dock soccer leagues existed from the USSR to Australia to Brazil to England. Although poorly recognized by soccer historians, dock soccer is an important, understudied cause of the rapid popularization of the sport in the early 1900s.

The first recorded game of dock soccer in Louisiana was between two British ships, the *Leland* and *Harrison*. Officers and engineers from those two ships played their game in Audubon Park. Moreover, this is the first recorded soccer game in Audubon Park, which became a hub for soccer all the way to 2000. Soccer was not welcome on many fields, often because football coaches did not want to share their grounds. Audubon was one of the few places soccer was welcome. As a result, Audubon Park's soccer fields became one of the most important locations for high school and club soccer in the 1960s and through the 1990s.

The 200 on-lookers who witnessed the British match were entertained, but confused since "soccer is unusual to New Orleans."

Clearly, soccer was not popular Uptown, and had not been since the early days of the YMGC. Even then, soccer was played only a few times in that section of New Orleans. *Harrison* defeated *Leyland* 11-1 and was awarded a large box of candy, presented by one of the lady viewers.

Soccer Football Played By Britons At Audubon Park

There have been "pick-up" team games by the crews of ships in port, long before this in New Orleans. But Sunday was the first real Inter-Line match.

P. S. Barrow, third officer of the steamship Discoverer, was captain of the victorious Harrison Line team, which was made up of picked players from the officers and crews of the two Harrison line steamers, Actor and Discoverer now in port.

A. Malabar, third engineer on the Oxonian, was the captain of the Leyland Line team. His men were picked from the crews of the Leyland Line steamers Oxonian and Alexandrian.

More than 200 rooters from the British colony in New Orleans cheered the game. Miss Daisy Anderson, of New Orleans, awarded a huge box of candy to the winners. Some recognition of this honor was required. So Miss Anderson was given the honor of kicking off. Which she did to the cheers of both teams and rooters.

The New Orleans Item, October 20, 1919.

Orleanians displayed a keen interest in a game of Soccer football played at Audubon Park Sunday afternoon by two teams composed of officers and engineers from the British steamships Leland and Harrison. Harrison won the game, 10 to 1, completely outclassing the opponents.

Soccer is unusual to New Orleans and many spectators demanded an explanation of what it was. When advised, their interest perked up and they stuck until the timekeeper blew the last whistle. A game of baseball in progress on the same field lost its crowd to the Soccer game.

The series of Soccer games have been arranged by the British Service Club for the entertainment of crews from British ships visiting New Orleans. The American mind saw something funny in the skillful manner in which the Britons bounced the ball with head and "tummy," and also the wonderful footwork. Both teams played splendid ball, considering they were composed of seafaring men who do not get much leg exercise except for shifting the knee cap to suit the bounding wave.

The Times Picayune, October 20, 1919.

A similar scenario played out on Christmas Eve, 1921. This time it was the British cruiser *Constance*. Teams from the ship were formed. One game was played Christmas Eve at Audubon Park. A second game was played at the park on Christmas. On Boxing Day, a third game was to be played at Tulane Stadium. Mayor Andrew McShane, son of two Irish Catholic immigrants, received the officers of the ship. It is unlikely but unknown if McShane played or was a fan of soccer. It is likely, however, that McShane was the first mayor of New Orleans to attend a soccer match.

MAYOR TO RECEIVE BRITISH OFFICERS

Three Games of Soccer on Program for Crew of Cruiser Constance.

Officers of the British cruiser Constance will be received by Mayor McShane and other city officials at a public reception Saturday morning at 11 o'clock.

Following the reception, two teams from the Constance will play a game of soccer football in Audubon Park. The match will start at 2:30 o'clock. After the game a committee appointed by Mayor McShane will entertain the officers at a banquet in the Louisiana Restaurant.

Sunday afternoon teams from the ship will play a second game of soccer in Audubon Park, starting at 2:30 o'clock. Another game will be staged in the Tulane stadium Monday afternoon at the same hour. The games will decide the championship of teams made up from the crew of the boat. Monday night the officers will be entertained at a reception and dinner by Mr. and Mrs. C. B. Fox at the Louisiane. The Constance will leave New Orleans Tuesday for Mobile, Ala.

Friday afternoon a reception was held in honor of the officers at the home of Mr. and Mrs. W. J. Bentley.

The Times Picayune, December 24, 1921.

Dock soccer gave a real international flavor to Louisiana soccer in the coming decades. Its existence would carry on until the 1980s at the least. The examination of *dock soccer* will continue, but not before we explore a new development in the local soccer scene in New Orleans: Central American soccer.

Central American soccer came to Louisiana thanks to the expansion of trade connecting Louisiana to Latin America that blossomed following World War I. This nexus led to the start of modern soccer in Louisiana. The contemporary high school and club soccer scene in Louisiana traces its history directly to this Latin American soccer.

1923-1925: Central American Soccer Arrives in Louisiana

The distance between New Orleans and Tegucigalpa, the capital of Honduras, is approximately 1000 miles. The distance is shorter than that between New Orleans and Washington D.C., Monroe and Chicago, Lake Charles and Miami, and Shreveport and Denver. That geographic proximity connected Louisiana to Central America in ways that changed the histories of both regions and the world forever during the Cold War. One of the minor side effects of that connection between the two regions was the reintroduction of soccer in Louisiana. It was the Latin American exportation of soccer that would lay the foundations for the modern game of soccer that exists to this day.

Filibusters are people who invade nations without approval from their native nation. These military campaigns are unauthorized invasions, usually for the purpose of wealth accumulation, but sometimes, simply for the purpose of adventure. In the 1850s, Louisiana and Texas were hotspots for American filibuster campaigns into Mexico, Nicaragua, Honduras, Guatemala, and Cuba. Certain Southerners, like William Walker, wanted land.

When gold was discovered in California, Walker knew that the quickest way to get people and supplies from the East to California was not over land, but by ship. Many had explored the idea of building a canal through the isthmus of Central America to create an easy route from the Atlantic to the Pacific. The machinery of the time made such a bold plan possible for the first time in history.

The motive and the tools were there. Others, however, owned that land. So the filibusters, infused with and inspired by the philosophy of Manifest Destiny, invaded Central American countries, hoping to seize that land and build a connecting waterway that would lead them to enormous fortunes.

The filibustering campaigns were, for those who partook in them, failures. The Honduran government, for instance, executed Walker. Southern attention shifted away from Central America because the lock step march toward civil war had already begun.

After the Civil War, the banana trade was dominated by the big Northeastern cities. That changed as a result of several individuals in New Orleans, namely the Vaccaro brothers, whose company would become the Standard Fruit Company (and later, Dole), and Sam Zemurray, owner of what would become the United Fruit Company (and later, Chiquita).

The banana trade that connected Louisiana to Central America was more than just an exchange of labor and goods for money. These banana companies essentially colonized the lands of Guatemala, Nicaragua, and Honduras. The numbers are staggering.

At its height, United Fruit owned more than 70 percent of private land in Guatemala and 50 percent in Honduras. The company employed more than 100,000 in Central America, working to produce a single crop that made up 90% of Honduran exports. The term *banana republic* developed in this time, and it suited the situation well.

United and Standard Fruit Companies wove the two regions together. In the early 20th century, many of the children of Latino employees were granted visas to study in Louisiana. The idea was not entirely noble.

The large fruit companies knew that the long-term success of their companies required an educated, bi-lingual segment of the Central American population. Holy Cross High School in the lower 9th Ward welcomed a good number of these students as boarders. LSU and Tulane were also common destinations for the more well to do children of Central of America. Lured by better economic prospects, many of these students chose to stay in Louisiana once their time in school was completed.

Soccer was already a game that two generations of Hondurans and Guatemalans knew, as it had begun in these nations in the 1890s. At first, only the wealthy in Central America played soccer. By 1917, however, soccer eclipsed baseball as the most popular sport in the region. The famous Honduran club, Club Deportivo Olimpia, the namesake of one of the most important squads in Louisiana history, started in 1912.

Most of the Central American boarders and college students who came to Louisiana during this period were affluent in their home countries. Most also played soccer, and, not surprisingly, they brought the game of soccer with them.

They must have been surprised to find that soccer did not exist in Louisiana. Little would they have known about Louisiana's long soccer history. Although soccer was introduced and played in Louisiana before it was in Central America, by the time this new wave of immigration came ashore, local soccer was lost to history and perhaps stories told in the pubs of the Irish Channel.

The first Latin American team in Louisiana was the Guatemala Soccer Club. Although an exact year of founding is unknown, its founding was no later than 1923. 1923 was also the year of founding for the New Orleans Soccer Club (NOSC), a club that had a long and impressive history. Its membership initially was about half Latin, but over the decades, it would become predominantly a Central American soccer team.

The local press seemed to be genuinely interested in the game during this time. It had been more than a generation since the professional New Orleans Football Association League failed. Few people remembered how soccer had once been quite popular in the city. Even the local sports press forgot. In fact, the writer for *The Times Picayune* in 1924 identified the NOSC as "the first soccer club formed in this city." His mistake was not the first or the last when it came to making superlatives about soccer in Louisiana. Ignorance about the game's history in Louisiana was and is the norm, even within the soccer community.

Soccer Football Club Organized

Local soccer football enthusiasts held a meeting Friday evening for the purpose of organizing a soccer football club, to be called the New Orleans Soccer Club. The new organization plans to play games every Sunday afternoon at Audubon Park.

Today the club meets the Guatemala Soccer Club, which at present is in this city. Play will commence at 2:45 o'clock.

Members of the club are all residents of New Orleans and are: R. Loyal, captain; W. Marks, secretary and treasurer; L. Scott, A. Ashby, A. Fano, P. Casado, F. Casado, J. Martinez, R. Brierly, J. Walsh, A. Anderson, J. Middleton, A. Jimenez, J. Betrane, A. Cruz, J. Answatagee, E. Soleria.

All communications should be addressed to W. Marks, 2501 Dryades street, or phone Jackson 3170.

The Times Picayune, December 23, 1923.

R. Loyal served as the first captain of the New Orleans Soccer Club. Their games were held at Audubon Park. In the club's first game, both Guatemala and NOSC scored two goals, with the captain of the Guatemalan team, Chapparito Figueredo, having noteworthy play. The NOSC sharpened its skill with dock soccer as well. In its inaugural season, the club played several teams composed of sailors from visiting ships (*The Times Picayune*, Feb. 17, Mar. 19, Mar. 25, and Apr. 18, 1924).

A week after the New Orleans Soccer Club's start, LSU began its first soccer team. Under the direction of Coaches Mike Donahue and Leo Morey, star of soccer teams in Peru and the Mira Flores Athletic Club, the team held tryouts. They hoped to play against some of the "professional" teams that apparently existed in New Orleans. The term *professional* was likely used very loosely. When LSU later played New Orleans area teams, it was usually crew ship teams or teams like the NOSC.

L. S. U. Planning to Have Strong Soccer Team

Baton Rouge, La., Jan. 8.—For the first time in history of the university soccer will be included among the sports at L. S. U. This comes as a result of Mike Donahue's intensive interest as athletic director of the Gold and Purple.

Leo Morey, South American soccer star and former captain of the Tumaculada college of Lima, Peru, and the Mira Flores Athletic Club teams, will have charge of coaching duties. It is planned for each company in the cadet battalion to have a team, and games will be arranged among the five companies.

After the conclusion of these games, the leading players from each team will be picked and formed into a team and Coach Donahue hopes to schedule a game with one of the professional teams of New Orleans and also a return game.

The Times Picayune, January 9, 1924.

LSU's team gathered for the first time in March of 1924. Over sixty students met at the Parade Grounds on campus. In the shadow of the school's majestic Campanile, Coach Donahue chose the best of the crop. Chief among those to make the cut were "several of the South American students who have had experience in the game abroad" (*The Times Picayune*, March 28, 1924).

The New Orleans Soccer Club, pictured below, was a great team. In fact, the local press crowned the team "Champion Soccer Team of Dixie" in the Spring of 1924. The squad defeated Holy Cross amongst others. Holy Cross fielded a team for much of the 1920s (Allan Shuford, "A History of Holy Cross Tiger Soccer: A Perspective. LAprepSoccer).

The Times Picayune, May 18, 1924
From left to right, back row: C. Wals, B. Martinez, G. Reid.
Center row: W. Marks (secretary); T. Landells, H. Loyal (captain), J. Middleton, C. Solera.
Front row: A. Jimenez, G. Answatagee, P. Casado.

NOSC's dominance continued into the Fall of 1924. Teams played included the following crew ship teams: *Creoles*, the *Defenders*,

Steamships *Win* and *Worron*, the Norwegians, the *Oranians*, and the British ship *Calcutta*, and Holy Cross. Games were played in Audubon Park, the Marine Hospital on Tchoupitoulas and Henry Clay, and the downtown campus of Holy Cross. After an undefeated Autumn season, the NOSC went undefeated again in the Spring of 1925, beating the *Creoles* 2-0, Holy Cross 6-1, *Defenders* 4-2, and *Win* and *Worron* 2-0.

Another very important development in Louisiana soccer in the 1920s was the introduction of girls soccer. With the leadership of Florence Smith, the Young Women's Christian Association (YWCA) fielded two teams that played each other. This first ever Louisiana girls soccer game was played on November 15, 1924 in City Park. Two YWCA teams participated. There is evidence that soccer was played by members of the YWCA through at least 1930. The majority of these players had Anglo-Saxon surnames like Walsh, Robinson, and McDonough.

Fair Sex Soccer Teams Formed by Y.W.C.A.

What are the fair sex athletes going to do next?

The Young Women's Christian Association, through Miss Florence Smith, physical instructor of the above organization, has introduced soccer for girls in the city of New Orleans. A splendid field has been laid out at City Park and every Sunday afternoon the girls gather and have real honest-to-goodness soccer games, just the same as the rough and tumble affair the men indulge in.

The first game was held last Saturday afternoon, with the Whites defeating the Reds by a score of 2 to 0. The score, however, does not indicate the closeness of the game. The weather is yet too warm for soccer, but just as soon as it gets cooler there will be some snappy games among the misses. Miss Smith is very enthusiastic over the interest the girls are displaying in their new enterprise, and she hopes to have three or four teams organized in the gym class, these teams meeting each other in order to make the game still more interesting.

The following have been reporting each week and have been taking part in the various games: Misses R. Pastorek, A. Pastorek, Zern, Robinson, Walsh Fischer, Helen Thatcher, Lucille Thatcher, Schwartz, White, the McDonogh twins, Kron, Clifford, Tallo and a number of others.

The Times Picayune, November 17, 1924

The soccer scene in New Orleans had recovered from the doldrums of the 1910s. A very strong club team existed in the NOSC. Holy Cross had a high school team. Girls were playing with the YWCA. Upstate, LSU had started a team.

A concrete way to know how successful soccer was is by looking at store advertisements in papers at the time. By 1926, soccer balls made their way to Canal Street, sold next to footballs, basketballs, and boxing gloves at Para's, "The Store that Guarantees Everything." Soccer boots were also showing up in the papers. The Uruguayan squad had just won the Olympics soccer title in 1925 when Keds paid for a full-page advertisement to showcase this shoe, worn by every member of the South American team.

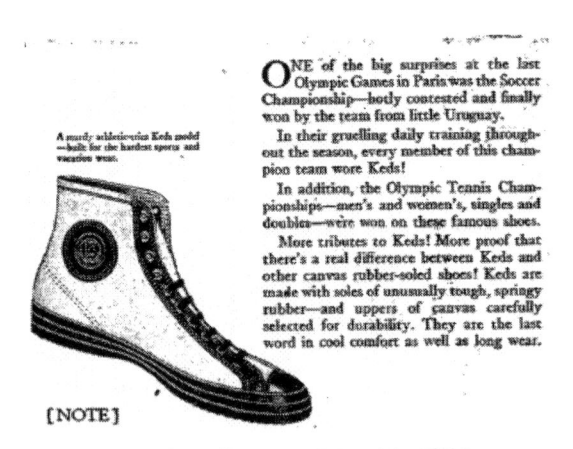

[NOTE]

The Times Picayune, May 28, 1925

Even with these advancements the sport struggled to attract a large, native-born following. New Orleans, indeed, Louisiana, was in love with a new passion by 1925: high school football. The famed Jesuit and Holy Cross rivalry began in 1922, and would reach its peak in 1940 when over 34,000 gathered at Tad Gormley Stadium to watch a game. Warren Easton also becomes a football rivalry of both Jesuit and Holy Cross as well. Warren Easton's largest games were preceded by a large parade down Canal Street, witnessed by thousands each year. Football was Louisiana's sport. Soccer in Louisiana was destined to remain an immigrant game played near the port for several decades.

1926-1949: German and Latino Soccer Rules the State

While New Orleans soccer consisted mostly of a few small clubs and crews from foreign ships in port, soccer in St. Louis, Chicago, New Jersey, and New York continued to grow in the late 1920s. A match in New York between a local team and a Viennese team drew 30,000 spectators.

The Times Picayune, April 29, 1926.

There is no record of New Orleans soccer teams playing from the Spring of 1926 through the Fall of 1927, but it is likely clubs continued their competitions. Soccer reappeared in the papers during the Winter of 1928. The only game recorded for that season was a 1-1 tie between NOSC and the British ship, *Matador*.

Latin teams like LSU, the New Orleans Soccer Club, and Guatemala continued playing, usually unreported by the press, through the 1920s and early 1930s. Soccer was a constant near the ports, but besides that, soccer was off the radar screen of most people in New Orleans and Louisiana.

Tulane's team had ceased to exist by 1933. When sailors from the H.M.S. *Norfolk* gathered near Tulane Stadium, a group from the student body and the football team gathered to watch (photo below). Unaccustomed to the game, one of the football players called the sport, "interesting."

The Times Picayune, March 14, 1933

The state of soccer in New Orleans was so barren in 1934 that when the HMS *Danae* arrived in the city in February, the city's welcoming committee asked the Times Picayune to seek any soccer teams "if there are any." The committee was hoping to provide a soccer game for the *Danae*'s crew team. Ultimately, no teams stepped forward, so the crew split to form two teams in order to play (*The Times Picayune*, March 6, 1934).

It was perhaps that failure to field a team that inspired members of the German American civic group, the Deutsches House, to organize a team in 1934. The team's name was Football Club Germania (F.C. Germania). President of the club was Bernhard M. Linemann. Germania's first season consisted of playing visiting German sailors. During World War II, the pre and post-game activities shared between certain members of F.C. Germania and crews of the visiting German ships caught the attention of federal investigators. These investigations culminated in a trial against one of F.C. Germania's leaders.

In the years that followed 1934, Germania played weekly games against a series of ships from throughout the world. Some of the ships Germania faced included the S.S. *Haimon*, *Eifel* (6-2), *Vosgesen*, *Vogeceu*, *Contessa* & *Granada*, the Norwegian *America* motorship, and the Swedish *Uddeholm* (6-2). From February of 1934 to January, 1935, F.C. Germania went 23-3-2. Games were played in City Park.

It is unknown what became of the New Orleans Soccer Club of the previous decade. It did not exist by the time of F.C. Germania's founding. F.C. Germania successful play attracted the attention of more than a few locals. The team's success led to an increase in popularity of the game. It also led to a second Germania squad forming in 1935. These two teams were the only known local soccer teams in Louisiana during this period. It is probable that Latin American immigrants formed teams that played at this time, but there is no record of them.

F. C. Germania, New Orleans' Only Soccer Football Team

F. C. Germania of the Deutsches Haus is the only soccer team from the city of New Orleans. It was started in February of 1934 and has played 28 games, its opponents being members of visiting ships. Of the 28 battles, 23 have been won, three tied and two lost. The entire team is shown above. From left to right, front, are B. Linemann, J. Junius; kneeling, F. de la Reguera, R. Castro, A. Junius, J. Eirich, E. Wetzell; standing, C. Sutter, president; A. Merkel, H. Vahrenhorst, captain; O. Labiltzke, O. Spiess and R. Esquivel.

The Times Picayune, February 10, 1935.

Here Are New Orleans' Only Two Soccer Football Teams

Above is shown the only soccer football teams in the city. When first organized, from among members of the Deutsches Haus, a local German organization, the club had but a bare 11 members. It has grown now to an outfit with two full teams. The two elevens will play an intraclub contest today at 4 p. m., at City Park. From left to right they are, reclining, J. Junius and L. Castro; middle row: F. Krause, B. Carrizos, R. Esquivel, E. Castro, J. Gutierrez, Al Junius, A. Coelo and J. Eirich; top row: F. Nishi, referee; B. Linemann, H. Vahrenhorst, E. Wetzel, E. Rompf, G. West, De Montasenteau, P. Goldup, B. Coelo, B. Gerharht, G. Esquivel, Al Merkel, F. de la Reguera and C. Sutter, manager.

The Times Picayune, May 26, 1935.

117

F.C. Germania existence is the first evidence of German Americans playing soccer in Louisiana since the Grand German Volkfests of the 1870s. Initially, the team was predominantly German. There were a couple of Latino players in the early years, but a decade later, Latinos would predominate the F.C. Germania team. The initial roster is as follows: J. Junius (goal keeper), Wetzel and Reguera (fullbacks), Gerhardt, Nogueria, and A. Junius (halfbacks), and Castro, Merkel, and Hubert Vahrenhorst (forwards). Vahrenhorst served as captain (*The Times Picayune*, April 15, 1934). Mr. C. Sutter managed the Deutsches Haus' two soccer squads.

1934 also marked the United States' return to the World Cup. In 1930, the U.S. placed third in the inaugural World Cup, without receiving any media attention in Louisiana. The papers in New Orleans four years later, however, made sure the people of this land knew about this squad. Below is a picture from *The Times Picayune* showing the American squad preparing for their match against Italy in the opening round of the sixteen-team tournament. The U.S. squad was a late entry into the 1934 World Cup. The team formed late, and did not draw from the top players in America. In fact, during a tune-up game, the U.S. team lost 4-0 to the American League All Stars. The national team consisted mostly of players from New York and St. Louis. The talent scouts certainly did not visit the South. That limited talent pool led to a quick exit for the U.S. squad. Italy easily dispatched the Americans, 7-1, and went on to win the Cup in Rome.

Soccer football requires headwork, and above are four of Uncle Sam's hopes at skull practice. The American players were snapped during a practice session in Philadelphia just before the squad sailed for Rome to compete for the world championship. They are, left to right: Fiedler, Gallagher, Lehman and Nilson.

The Times Picayune, May 10, 1934

By 1936, F.C. Germania had become predominantly Latino. Cuba, Honduras, Nicaragua, Guatemala and Mexico were represented on the team. It was still captained by a German, Captain Vahrenhorst, however. Hubert Vahrenhorst was an enthusiastic promoter of the game, and "urged all local clubs and organizations to form teams so that a league may be composed" (*The Times Picayune*, April 26, 1936).

As New Orleans drew more Latino residents, the popularity of soccer expanded. Some of these new residents took up Vahrenhorst's call to form new teams. A third team, this time entirely Latino, was organized as the Latino Tigers, and possibly was linked to Holy Cross High. The Tigers played their first game against F.C. Germania on April 26, 1936. That game was the first of many games against the two squads.

They Want Victory Over Rival Soccer Team

The Times Picayune, May 9, 1937

In the coming decades, Hispanic soccer in Louisiana grew to include more than just the Tigers. The new Hispanic teams competed against each other, teams from visiting ships, and, often, against one team made up of a conglomerate of European expats living in New Orleans.

The F.C. Germania and Latino Tiger rivalry also gave us the first action shot from a local game published in a local paper. In that match, F.C. Germania defeated the Tigers 3-0 in City Park, where most games in this period were held.

Hubert Socked It, But Goalie Blocked It

> —Photo by The Times-Picayune.
> Hubert Vahrenhorst, center forward of the Germania soccer football team, is pictured here just before he planted a boot in the ball for an unsuccessful try at a goal. However, the Germania team came back later to defeat the Latino Tigers by a score of 3 to 0 Sunday afternoon at City Park.
> The teams battled on even terms for 70 minutes before Germania scored the only points of the game during the last 10 minutes of play. R. Esquivel and Captain Albert Merkel made the markers. Esquivel tallied twice for the winners while Merkel added the other point on a shot through the uprights.
> Germania and the Latino Tigers are the only soccer football teams in the city.

The Times Picayune, March 23, 1937.

The two squads, one Latino and one German, created interest in the sport hereto unseen in Louisiana. Beginning in 1937, the teams would occasionally put together an all-star squad. This squad then challenged the teams of visiting crew ships, which by this time had become very competitive. The dominance the early F.C. Germania squads saw was soon to end.

On Boxing Day, 1937, a team of the best from the Latin Tigers and F.C. Germania battled the British cruiser, H.M.S. *Orion*. The British sailors proved too strong, winning 7-0 before an estimated crowd of 3000. The photo below shows S. Culotta of the Latino Tigers challenging H. Hambly of the *Orion* as the referee watches.

The Times Picayune, December 26, 1937.

That setback did not undermine the growing soccer interest in New Orleans. On February 28, 1938, the all-stars of New Orleans faced off against the Dutch ship, *Veendam*. Before a crowd estimated at 5,000 in Municipal Stadium, later renamed Tad Gormley Stadium, the Dutch squad downed the New Orleanians 3-0. It would be another 62 years before a soccer game in Louisiana drew that many people.

The fans of New Orleans were not only interested in the all-star matches against the visiting ships' crews. More than 3000 saw a game at City Park Stadium (a.k.a. Municipal Stadium) between the Latino Tigers and Germania. Germania captured the win, 2-0 (*The Times Picayune*, March

11, 1940). The Latino Tigers and Germania were highly competitive and neither team dominated the other. The year before Germania's 1940 city championship, the Latino Tigers defeated the Germans, 3-1 to capture the Montesanteu Cup and the city championship (*The Times Picayune*, March 14, 1939).

High school girls soccer saw its birth in 1938. Ursuline Academy, the oldest continuously operated school for females in America, founded in 1727, was the first school in Louisiana to participate in girls soccer. The Ursuline teams may be some of the first high school soccer girls teams in America. The soccer, however, was not interscholastic, and it may have been rudimentary. From 1938 through 1941, the Ursuline freshman, sophomores, juniors and seniors each fielded a team that competed.

Frosh, Sophs Meet Today for Ursuline Soccer Title

The freshman and sophomore teams of Ursuline college will meet for the championship of the college in the final game of the interclass soccer tournament today at 4:30 p. m. on the college court. Referee will be Miss Dorothy McCloskey, faculty director of athletics.

A decisive victory by the freshmen last Friday eliminated the junior team from the tournament. The senior class did not enter a team in the tournament because of scholastic conflicts.

The Times Picayune, April 4, 1938.

Also in 1937, the Newcomb College [Newcomb was merged with Tulane in 2006] girls fielded their first varsity team. It was not an interscholastic squad, however. The team only played Newcomb faculty members several times a year. The importance of this squad and of the high school ones is to show that girls were playing soccer in Louisiana very early on. They played before softball and volleyball. Soccer was one of the earliest sports females in Louisiana regularly played.

Tulane's men's team did not exist during most of the 30s and 40s. However, there was soccer played at Tulane. Claude "Big Monk" Simons, the famed trainer at Tulane, in an interview on August 1 of 1943, said, "I didn't coach soccer for a varsity team because we had no soccer competition, but that sport was also included in my athletic program at Tulane at some time or another."

Louisiana girls soccer began with the Young Women's Christian Association (YWCA) in 1924. The YWCA held semi-competitive games at camps through the 1920s. Perhaps some of these girls matriculated a decade later at Newcomb College in New Orleans. In 1937, thirteen years after the YWCA introduced soccer to females in Louisiana, Newcomb College began offering the sport in the Fall to its students. A year later, Ursuline Academy, the oldest Catholic school in America, just a couple blocks from Newcomb, offered soccer to its female students in 1938.

LSU's men's soccer team followed a similar timeline as the early women's soccer game in Louisiana. After being founded in 1924, the LSU team does not show up again in the papers until 1938. When LSU's team does reappear it does so with a new name: the Colon team. This name was likely borrowed from the famed Argentine club team or a league that existed in Honduras.

The Colon team at LSU was not a varsity sport, as we would use the term today. It was a club sport. Its players were mostly Latino. The teams played most of their matches against fellow LSU squads, usually on the Parade Grounds near the majestic oaks of Highland Road. Occasionally, the teams played in Tiger Stadium before LSU football games. One such game, on November 1, 1947, before the LSU-Ole Miss game, was said to have been "worth half the price of admission."

Back in New Orleans, the Latino Tigers were forming quite the rivalry with the LSU team. The Latino Tigers, which sometimes used the team name of the old New Orleans Soccer Club, may have been associated with the Holy Cross neighborhood. The Latino Tigers won the first match against LSU, 6-1, in April of 1938. LSU would make a return trip to City Park's Municipal Stadium shortly after Christmas of the same year. This time, the Colon squad defeated F.C. Germania 1-0. Interestingly, Germania played with H. Clark and S. Venegas, two students from the University of Iowa.

On June 26, 1939, the first game on the Westbank of New Orleans was played. The newly organized Behrman Memorial Life Guards played the Brazilian crew of the *Alegrete* to a 1-1 draw. The game was held at Behrman Memorial Park. The Berhman Memorial Life squad was not the only team trying to start playing regular games in this period. In 1941, the barbers of New Orleans, organized by Johnny Lascola, sought to form a team that would play games at City Park (*T.P.* 9/7/1941).

The anti-soccer movement in America had not yet begun during the World War II days. Tank men at Camp Livingston, just north of Pineville, started a soccer league. The reasoning behind the formation of the league: a new motto: Get Tough. Soccer was still seen as a manly, tough sport. "Soccer, you'll remember, is no game for sissies," wrote the *Times Picayune* reporter (October 28, 1942).

"Get Tough" was not the only thing the war brought with it. Throughout the States, xenophobia spread. In New Orleans, the large German-American population felt the brunt of it. Hubert Vahrenhorst, one of the founders of F.C. Germania and one of the leading proponents of soccer in Louisiana during the 1930s, faced having his citizenship revoked.

Vahrenhorst's meetings with German ships, whose crews he played in soccer matches, was the weight of the evidence against him. According to prosecutors, Vahrenorst boarded German ships in guise of preparing for soccer matches. The real reason the prosecutors said he boarded the ships was to retrieve German literature and German flags. In short, he was accused of being a spy for the Nazis.

Forced to make account of the F.C. Germania, Vahrenorst told the court the ethnic origins of the team. His testimony showed that the members of the team were Latino, one was Turkish, and four were German. When forced to account for a flag in his possession, Vahrenorst said it was a black and gold pennant with the letters FCG. A cook on one of the ships gave it to him to celebrate the New Orleans F.C. Germania. The court acquitted Vahrenorst, but the trial left its mark on him and the sport. Soccer more than ever before was locally viewed as a foreigner's sport.

While college soccer, girls soccer, and local New Orleans soccer existed in New Orleans in the late 1930s, dock soccer continued its sporadic yet intense presence after World War II. Near the end of the European campaign, British and Argentine crews faced each other in City Park (*The Times Picayune*, March 30, 1945).

Norwegian ships regularly docked in New Orleans and participated in dock soccer. However, beginning in 1945, local Norwegian Christian communities began contributing to the organization of the game. For instance, the Norwegian Seamen's Mission, which is still in operation today, and the Seamen's Bethel, organized matches between crews from Norwegian, Argentine and British ships in City Park (*The Times Picayune*, July 25, 1945).

While the city provided the sailors with a field for their games, the crews gave back to the city. Besides the free entertainment provided, the Norwegian ship Rio Nova gave the Audubon Zoo a baby puma to add to its collection. The puma, which the ship got in Mexico, was the soccer team's mascot, but had since grown too large for the ship. The Audubon Zoo was all too happy to take it.

The Times Picayune, October 7, 1945.

In February of 1947, for the first time since 1941, a New Orleans soccer team played a public exhibition. The new team was named the

International Soccer Ball Club (ISBC). The coach? Surprisingly, Hubert Vahrenhorst, the same Hubert Vahrenhorst of F.C. Germania who the federal government tried to send back to Germany in 1943.

Vahrenhorst and the club seem to distance themselves from the Deutsches Haus and the former F.C. Germania, claiming that this new team is a rebranding of the Latino Tigers, who won the last New Orleans championship in 1941. Decked in blue and white striped uniforms, their first game was against the Swedish cruiser *Gotland*. The visitors won 5-0.

The ISBC slated several games in the following months against visiting cruisers. Two weeks later the International Soccer Ball Club faced Argentine ship *Rio Deseado* at City Park. In March, they faced the French *Jeanne d'Arc*. Referees for the matches at City Park alternated between Coach Vahrenhorst and officers from the visiting ship. Either international soccer had grown up or the local team just was not very good. The ISBC lost every publicized match that year. Soccer in Louisiana fell further behind football, basketball, and baseball.

1950-1958: Clubs and Colleges Converge in League Play

Entering the 1950s, soccer was unorganized in Louisiana, but interest was on the increase. The international club game grew very quickly in antebellum Europe. The confederation of ship crew teams that played in New Orleans expanded. With weekly games, the visiting crews formed a version of a traveling league. Games were constant; teams were not. What kept the league intact and formed was the Norwegian Seaman's Mission. As a result, 1950s New Orleans was home to an international amateur soccer league.

The International Soccer Ball Club, founded in 1947, morphed to become the New Orleans Soccer Club in September of 1949. The leaders of the New Orleans Soccer Club attempted to kick-start a city league, the first real go at it since the New Orleans Soccer League of 1907.

Leading members of the New Orleans Soccer Club included the following: President Carl Garmann; Vice President Roy Erving; Board Members Arne Futsaether and Erik Ruud.

Crescent City Group Organizes Club to Stimulate Soccer Interest

By BOB ROESLER

You might have seen a large group of men battling in out on the greens along Marconi dr. A good look probably brought the question "What are those guys doing?" The answer would be "playing soccer, of course!"

It seems as though this sport popular throughout many of these United States is catching on here in our Crescent City.

For some time now, seamen of various foreign merchant ships in port have been playing the game just about every Sunday. Through the co-operation and work of a group of Norwegians, facilities to and the game have been acquired.

Last September the New Orleans Soccer Club was formed. The object of the club is to spread knowledge and stimulate interest in soccer in the universities and colleges along the Gulf area.

At Tulane university there are 22 students that play the game and at Louisiana State university there are two complete teams. And just recently the collegians met a team from a Uruguayan ship, and humbled the South Americans.

To date, 80 matches have been played on the City Park soccer field with teams from Spain, Italy, Australia, Argentina, Sweden, Norway and Denmark participating.

The local soccer club, under the guidance of newly elected president Carl Garmann, is striving to form a league here in the New Orleans area. Other officers of the club, which include vice-president Roy Erving, board Arne Futsaether and Erik Ruud, have been working tirelessly to promote the sport.

Information of the proposed league, or questions about the sport may be obtained by writing Ebbe Stranges, Rom 506, International bldg.

The Times Picayune, October 13, 1950

College soccer continued at LSU and Tulane in the early 1950s. Only the intramural departments sponsored those soccer programs. Games were played at Audubon Park and the format was similar to football in that there were four quarters instead of halves, at least according to the media. The programs were evenly matched in the early 1950s.

By Spring of 1951, the first pan-Louisiana soccer league was formed. Member teams included Tulane A, Tulane B, the New Orleans Soccer Club, LSU, and Phi Iota Alpha. Phi Iota Alpha was a team of LSU students who were members of the Phi Iota Alpha fraternity. The fraternity is the nation's oldest Latino fraternity. LSU's chapter, established in 1931, boasts members who became the presidents of Honduras, Panama, and Columbia.

On April 8, 1951, the Times Picayune Dixie Magazine devoted three full pages to a story about the new soccer league. The story detailed the birth of the 1950 Tulane soccer team. Three students, one from the East Coast and two from South Africa approached a former Maryland soccer player, Lt. Logan, who was then a gunnery instructor for the Tulane ROTC. Logan agreed to coach and a team was formed. Like college club teams even to this day, there was a shoestring budget, but soccer, being cheaply organized, would be played. Among Tulane's best was Leif Kvumn, a Norwegian student (pictures on following pages).

The New Orleans Soccer Club came about because expats of many countries in New Orleans saw foreign crews playing soccer weekly on the fields of New Orleans. "Why not have a local team to play foreign ships when they come?" asked Arne Futsaether. Among the best of the

NOSC were Frank Narvorro of the Canary Islands, Erik Ruud of Norway, and Ratko Djokovich of Yugoslavia. Before the war, Narvorro was on a championship Japanese team. Ruud was on one of the top amateur teams in Mexico. Djokovich was a professional star in Chicago. With such great talent, the NOSC finished the 1950-1951 season with a record of 17-2-1, with a 4-1 loss to LSU.

Most of the league games were played in Audubon Park. Tulane played some of its games on the Tulane baseball field, across the street from old Tulane Stadium. On December 15, 1951, Tulane played its first game in Tulane Stadium in a 1-1 tie with NOSC.

The 1952 Tulane team was the most widely reported soccer team in Louisiana. As part of the Carnival Committee of New Orleans, Tulane played the British ship *Sheffield*, while the New Orleans Soccer Club played *Sheffield's* No. 2 team in Tulane Stadium. Lief Kvamme of Tulane was described as one of the best players in all of college. The Tulane team also tried to schedule a game against national number two, Penn State.

If Tulane played Penn State, it was not reported. However, during some point of the Spring of 1952, LSU played PSU. Coaching PSU was William Jeffrey, legendary coach of the 1950 U.S. National Team that upset England 1-0 in the World Cup. Jeffrey was also winner of ten national soccer championships as coach at PSU. Jeffrey said that LSU's team, an all-Latino team, had "some of the best soccer material in the country" (*The Times Picayune*, May 3, 1952). Later in the season, LSU defeated Tulane 4-1 at this game held in Tiger Stadium.

Tulane soccer team lines up at makeshift goals erected on edge of baseball field. Lt. Edwin Logan (holding ball) is faculty adviser to unofficial group

Arno Cahn of the New Orleans Soccer Club tries to dispossess Leif Kvumn, Tulane's center forward who played the game in Norway.

Norwegians living in New Orleans had a pivotal role in organizing soccer in the 1950s. On July 22, 1951, the Norwegians formed their own team, the Norwegian Tigers under Coach Wangberg. The team had three former professionals on it. Even with that talent, the New Orleans Soccer Club was victorious in its first game against the Norwegian Tigers. The game ended 3-0 "before a capacity crowd at Audubon Park."

Boys youth soccer had very humble origins in Louisiana during this time as well. The first mention of boys youth soccer in Louisiana since the 1800s comes from an article about YMCA activities in 1951. The YMCA held camps in the summer in City Park (T.P. 8/12/1951). At these camps, soccer was played at least through 1959.

In the Fall of 1953, the new Gulf Coast Soccer League was formed. Bill Sloshberg, head of soccer at Tulane, was elected league president. The first teams in the league were Tulane, LSU, Regal Soccer Club, Fortier High School, and making a reappearance, the F.C. Germania.

Regal Soccer Club grew out of the New Orleans Soccer Club and split into A and B squads. The A team won 55 matches in a row before falling in the final against LSU 2-3 in the championship match at Audubon Park in May of 1954. As a result of the win, LSU was hailed as the "Southern soccer champion of the United States."

The Regal first squad was without question the top club in Louisiana through the 1950s and likely had international level talent on the squad. In a three-year stretch ending in 1954, the club's record was

320-4! Two of those losses came to rival LSU, also one of the best squads in the South. Regal's record against LSU during that time was 5-2.

The Regal teams were as cosmopolitan as they come. 21 nationalities were represented in the 1950s. Among those nations were Mexico, Honduras, Guatemala, Columbia, Nicaragua, Venezuela, Brazil, Chile, Argentina, Norway, Italy, France, Spain, Germany, Cuba, Ecuador, Austria, Denmark, and Sweden.

One notable game of this league was played on February 27, 1954. In it, the Regal Soccer Club scored a thrilling 6-2 victory over an aggregate team from Chicago. The Regal Soccer Club played several interstate games, including a game against the Dallas Soccer Club, champions of Texas in 1954.

Most games of this league were between foreign ships, and those games were usually held at Audubon Park. Other venues were Delgado Park and Algiers Memorial Stadium. Games regularly drew crowds of 300 to 400 spectators.

Perhaps most interesting of all in this league was the inclusion of a high school, Fortier. Fortier was an uptown New Orleans public school that closed after Hurricane Katrina. With some controversy, Lusher Charter School moved into Fortier's building in 2006, effectively marking the end of Fortier High School and its long soccer history.

Fortier began its soccer program in March of 1954 with the Gulf Coast Soccer League under the direction of Jose Veiga, a member of the Regal team. Fortier was the state's third high school program and first since the 1920s. As soccer was not recognized as a high school sport yet, and regulations did not exist, the Regal team used the Fortier squad as a farm system. The best of Fortier would graduate to one of the Regal teams.

March 15, 1955 marks an important date in Louisiana high school soccer history. On that date on the Audubon Park soccer field, Fortier and Country Day, coached by Chuck Miller, played in the first truly interscholastic high school soccer game in Louisiana. Holy Cross and Sacred Heart played a match in 1905, but it is uncertain if both teams were what we would today call high schools. Some players in that 1905 game may have been college students. In this match, Fortier defeated Country Day 2-0. The teams played three days later, ending in a 1-0 victory for the Tarpons of Fortier.

In 1955 was also the year that F.C. Germania was organized again for the first time since 1940. F.C. Germania played with the Bertucci brothers and Frank Navarro. This Germania squad did not equal the glory of its namesake. In its first game back, Germania lost to Regal A 9-1.

In 1956, the Gulf Coast Soccer League added Dima to its membership. Dima was a group of "former European soccer men." Other teams included LSU, Tulane, and Regal.

Coverage of state soccer disappeared in 1956 and did not return until the Spring of 1957 when LSU and the New Orleans Soccer Club played at Delgado. *The Times Picayune* did report on soccer -- international soccer. However, from the mid to late 50s, most of the soccer headlines were negative. The local media's focus on soccer turns from reporting on local matches to reporting eye-catching headlines about soccer fans rioting in Europe and South America as well as Soviet domination of the sport.

The local media joined with Southern college football coaches in speaking and writing about soccer in the pejorative.

These are the first negative descriptions of the game in local media. They would not be the last. During the 1960s, football coaches in the South continued the assault on soccer. Insults usually connected soccer to Communism, lack of American loyalty, and effeminacy. Behind the insults, perhaps, was a fear that soccer would steal players from the game of football. Not only that, soccer was the only other major sport that might share the football field. Basketball and baseball had their own venues. Soccer teams often sought to play its games on football fields.

Igniting the anti-soccer movement in Louisiana and in rest of the nation was the re-emergence of soccer as a potentially big sport in America in the late 1950s. For instance, in 1959, the NCAA sanctioned a men's soccer championship. In the 1960s, the North American Soccer League began, drawing some of the world's biggest names like Pelé to the American pitch. American football's bailiwick was threatened.

1959-1969: Carlos Ross Mitchell, ISLANO, and the New Orleans Timbers?

Louisiana soccer from the 1910s to 1960 had survived hanging by a thread. Although there were a couple of leagues through the decades, soccer still failed to capture the Louisiana imagination. By 1960, soccer was nearly exclusively known in Louisiana to Latino immigrants and the crews of visiting ships. One man, Carlos Ross Mitchell, tried to change that.

Mitchell was born in Tegucigalpa, Honduras in 1910. His father had moved to Honduras at the turn of the century to work as a U.S. Consular agent and pharmacist. In the fields of the lush, slopping hills, Mitchell learned the game of soccer. He probably was a fan of the local club team, Olimpia, and as a bright-eyed boy watched the fancy footwork of some of Central America's most talented players. At the age of 13, Mitchell and his family boarded a ship and moved to New Orleans.

When he arrived, he was disappointed to find that there were few soccer opportunities for teenagers like himself. Saddened by that, he endeavored to ensure that future children had opportunities to play soccer.

Soccer was an underground, or rather, a port-side sport in the late 1950s. It did not reappear in the public consciousness until 1960. That year a version of the Gulf Coast Soccer League, founded in 1953, reappeared as the Southern Soccer League. The league had a membership of mixed colleges in the region and a couple of New Orleans club teams.

At that time, LSU began a practice of having two club teams, one Purple and one Gold, a tradition that continued into the 1990s. Joining the LSU teams were squads from Tulane, University of Southwestern

Louisiana (USL, and later, ULL), and Mississippi Southern (USM). Southwestern Louisiana's team is the first known soccer team from that region of the state. New Orleans club teams included at least two Latino teams, America (America was probably a collection of Mexican expats who were fans of Club America in Mexico City) and Honduras.

The teams of the league continued the decades-old tradition of playing foreign ship teams. They would only play other league teams when foreign ship teams were unavailable. Games were held most often at Audubon Park, due to the park's history of being soccer friendly and its easy access to the ports of New Orleans.

The two club teams, America and Honduras, were founded before the 1960 league started through the auspices of the Club Deportivo Internacional (CDI). CDI was a Hispanic American organization founded in the 1950s that tried to strengthen Central American ethnic and cultural identity in New Orleans. The chief way it accomplished this goal was through the organization of soccer teams and the promotion of the sport to the Latino community in New Orleans.

Carolos Ross Mitchell was a chief figure in the CDI. It was through Mitchell's efforts that the Honduras squad formed in 1959. Mitchell was also responsible for the league getting and staying organized.

The league grew in the following seasons. By 1962, it consisted of both America and Honduras, the New Orleans Soccer Club, and college club teams from USL, USM, LSU, and Tulane. Membership in this league grew increasingly Latino as a result of the CDI's influence.

The Southern Soccer League started as a league dominated by college club teams. By 1963, however, thanks in large part to the Club Deportivo Internacional, the weight of the league rested with Hispanic club teams based in New Orleans.

The league was ready for a new name in 1963. Reflecting the truly international nature of the league, it took the name the International Soccer League of New Orleans (ISLANO). If that name sounds familiar, it should to local soccer aficionados. The league continues even today. ISLANO's membership roll shows that soccer in New Orleans was almost entirely Latino. Teams included were Honduras, America, Venezuela, Guatemala, Costa Rica, The Hub, and Holy Cross. Teams from LSU, Tulane, and Delgado Community College also participated.

In the Fall of that year, the league added several teams: Atletico and the Hammond Lions. It is unknown if this was a team associated with the University of Southeastern Louisiana (SLU). Nonetheless, it was the first recorded team from Hammond. Costa Rica defeated Honduras for the Fall 1963 title. Costa Rica's dominance continued into the Spring of 1964 when they won the league again (pictured on next page) and played for the title against LSU in 1965.

Although Tulane had been associated with various soccer leagues in New Orleans for two decades, it was noted that Tulane joined Islano in December of 1963. The team was managed by Chandler Knowles and coached by Kamal Zakhary. Most notably, the team's goalkeeper, Robert Mahfoud, was reported as being the keeper for the United Arab Republics (Egypt and Syria) at the 1956 Olympics.

CITY'S BEST—This is the America football team of the Club Deportivo Internacional, champions of the International Soccer League of New Orleans. Kneeling, from left: Guillermo Carcamo, Enrique Guadamud, Carlos Cordero, Rodolfo Mesorio, Edwin Morales and Guillermo Andrade. Standing: Coach Nigel Fraser, Salomon Andara, R. Varela Reyes, captain Eduardo Puente, Antonio Rodriguez, Hector R. Sanchez, Willis Waiton and Juan Villanueva.

The Times Picayune, April 7, 1963.

144

LSU's role in the league was important. Through the majority of the 1960s, LSU carried the banner of the best college team in Louisiana. LSU did not just stay in Louisiana, though. LSU, coached by A.L. Swanson, beat teams like Texas A&M, Florida State, Rice, and Mississippi Southern. The team, mostly Latino, but at times with players from China and Mauritius, also traveled abroad. A trip in 1967 to Nicaragua saw the Tigers lose to the Yucatan All-Stars and the University of Central America. More importantly, however, was the fact that Louisiana Governor John McKeithen and LSU President John Hunter traveled as ambassadors with the team. Their presence, though, did not lead to the formation of a varsity men's soccer program at LSU.

KINGPINS—This is the Costa Rica Soccer Club, champion of the International Soccer League of New Orleans. Shown kneeling, from left, are. Edwin Morales, captain; Jose Bonilla; Carlos Bonilla Sr.; Carlos Bonilla Jr.; Marco T. Mora and Oscar Bonilla, mascot. Standing, from left, are Jose Matarrita; Gilberto Ortiz; Ligia Ramirez, team sweetheart; Diego Povedano, Consul General of Costa Rica in New Orleans; Norman Kuylen; Carlos Hernandez; Jorge Morales; Milner DeLeon and Carlos R. Mitchell, president of the league.

The Times Picayune, April 13, 1964.

European expats also participated in the league. The European team was probably named The Hub, although that is unknown. In 1965, Ernest Seibel, captain of the European team of ISLANO, sought through the newspaper "experienced soccer players from Europe." His team already had players, "mostly Irish," but also from Germany, Austria, Hungary, France, and Britain. He sought more Europeans, however, in order to compete with the Latin American squads, which, in addition to the nationalities listed above, had players from Chile, Mexico, and Brazil. The European team played every Sunday at Audubon or along Lake Pontchartrain near the Coast Guard station.

Through the 1960s, the Hispanic teams of ISLANO dominated. A few of the publicized major happenings of ISLANO during the 1960s follows. In 1964 Honduras defeated Club Deportivo Internacional in the Casa Alejandro Cup Tournament. Two years later, Honduras defeated Costa Rica in the Mocambo Cup. Later that year, Honduras traveled to Houston to face Club Mexico, champions of the Texas State Soccer League. Team Honduras continued its impressive streak in 1967, defeating Ecuador for the league title at NORD Stadium. Honduras then played the college champion (unknown) for the state championship. Honduras won and played Texas champions, Club Mexico of Houston, at Jefferson Playground on April 2.

Carlos Ross Mitchell expanded the Honduras Soccer Club and founded the Olympia Soccer Club in 1966. He was named president for life of the club as well. Olympia was a power in both youth soccer and adult soccer through the 60s and the 70s.

Before high school soccer was more strictly regulated, teams not associated with schools were allowed to compete against school teams. During this brief period, the youth club of Olympia won three state championships and was runner-up once (1969-1972). Below is the 1968-1969 state champion Olympia youth squad.

SOCCER STYLE—Olympic Soccer Club of New Orleans won the junior cup championship of Louisiana. On the team were, from left, coach Guillermo Solis, Danilo Galindo, Michael Harmon, Maximo Harman, co-captain, Arturo Mejia, Jorge Barrera, Rodolfo Martinez, Mauricio Aguila, Oscar Tabora, Plutarco Trigueros and Carlos R. Mitchell, Louisiana junior commissioner.

The Times Picayune, May 11, 1969.

The Olympia adult team became a national force in the 1970s. In 1977, Olympia traveled to Philadelphia to participate in the U.S. Amateur Cup. The team fought hard, but lost 3-1 to the Arden Football Club of Pittsburg in the national quarterfinals. Another major accomplishment came in 1985. Olympia, playing with several UNO players, defeated Vienna Fortuna, a junior squad of the Bundesliga's Fortuna Düsseldorf.

Olympia was also responsible for setting up one of the biggest soccer matches in Louisiana history. In 2002, ISLANO leaders were able to bring the real Olimpia squad from Honduras to New Orleans. At the Tulane Soccer Field, Olimpia battled the Dallas Burn of the MLS. The game went to overtime, but no one scored. Penalty kicks came next, and the Burn escaped with the victory. It was a victory for Louisiana soccer, though, as two of the top teams in the Western Hemisphere met on the field in the Pelican State.

ISLANO is a strong force in Louisiana soccer even today. It has been a semi-professional league since the 1990s. Many Central American soccer stars have played in ISLANO. The players have not come to the city to play soccer. Like the British stars of the 1907 professional league, they came to find work. Playing soccer was something they did because they enjoyed it.

Several examples of this phenomenon were found in the ISLANO and LSA champions of 1996, Costa Rica. Martin Montero, a professional from Costa Rica, moved to New Orleans because the standard of living was greater in the Crescent City than in his home nation. He wanted his family to live more comfortably, so he brought them to New Orleans. When he discovered ISLANO he was thrilled to pick up his cleats again and take to the field. Walter Cortez of Costa Rica shared a similar experience., as did Kevin Edo. Edo, though, hailed from Nigeria. In Nigeria, he played for the U-21 Nigerian National Team (*T.P.*, 5/30/1996).

Many similar stories could be told through the years of ISLANO. There have been an untold number of former professional and national team members of Central and South American soccer teams that have played in ISLANO. One of the most famous may be Eduardo Antonio "Tony" Laing.

Mention the name Laing in Honduras and one is sure to get bright eyes and a smile. Rewind to the 1982 World Cup in Spain. Honduras qualified for the World Cup for the first time ever. After Honduras tied Spain 1-1, the Central American nation faced Northern Ireland. Moments after Laing entered the game, he scored a beautiful header off a corner (the goal is available on Youtube). Laing's goal was the last goal any Honduran has scored in a World Cup.

After the goal, Laing played professionally and coached in Honduras, but the pay was not great. He decided to move to America instead. While in America, he was offered to coach the Roma team in ISLANO. He took the job and has coached on Scout Island, City Park ever since (*The Times Picayune*, June 11, 2010).

ISLANO is still perhaps the best league in all of Louisiana. Large cash purses are yearly given to league winners, sometimes approaching $10,000. Attendance at the games in Pan American Stadium, City Park averages between 500 and 1000. Championship matches bring out huge Hispanic crowds.

Unfortunately for the game, ISLANO operated for many years separate from the Southeast Louisiana Adult Soccer Association (SELASA). SELASA, from its inception, has predominately been composed of Americans playing soccer. As a result, there has been a *de facto* segregation between the best American-born and immigrant soccer players in New Orleans for quite a while.

SELASA, however, has fielded some exceptional teams through the years. The league's dominant program has been Olympiakos Football Club, a squad that won seven championships in a row in the late 1990s and early 2000s (*The Times Picayune*, January 16, 2002). The team was founded by George Papapanagiotou and has always had a Greek American flavor. Olympiakos continues a long tradition of Greek American soccer in Louisiana. In 1983, the Greek-American Soccer Club of New Orleans (GASCNO) won the Region III tournament hosted at UNO. They defeated the North Texas Chiefs and advanced to Nationals in Dallas.

In recent years, Uptown United, Hellas United, and Finn McCool's, have challenged Olympiakos for dominance in SELASA. The Finn McCool's team, a team that derives from the Mid-City Irish pub of the same name, achieved some national recognition in 2009. That recognition was not for the team's soccer prowess. The team's fame came as a result of Stephen Rae's Katrina memoir, *Finn McCool's Football Club: The Birth, Death, and Resurrection of a Pub Soccer Team in the City of the Dead*.

The Finn McCool's pub, founded in 2002, has developed into a gathering place for soccer lovers, providing a soccer atmosphere that is reminiscent of that found in Britain and Ireland. The Londoner in Baton Rouge is another such pub. Both pubs represent a novel, European soccer culture that has swept through Louisiana, and indeed, the U.S. since the 2002 World Cup. One needs only to watch a Portland or Seattle MLS match to see this reflection of European soccer culture. In those stadiums and others throughout America, Euro-like songs are chanted and scarves are hoisted. This culture goes beyond the pitch: American television stations have signed large contacts foreign soccer leagues to bring that style into the homes and pubs of America.

The recent trend of Euro American soccer fans trying to emulate European soccer is a reflection of a larger shift in American soccer. U.S. soccer, for instance, has jettisoned the attempts to make a U.S. style of soccer – attempts to popularize high school and college soccer, create slightly different rules for American professional soccer, and develop an American style -- a philosophy that dominated in the 1990s. With the recent hiring of a foreign USMNT coach, American soccer, by and large, in both strategy and culture, has tried to mimic its European cousin rather than form its own.

Nonetheless, soccer remains a distinct sub-set of sports culture in America. While football, basketball, and baseball share a culture – part of the "major sports culture," soccer has remained apart, even as it has rivaled baseball in popularity, at least at the high school level. Soccer fans have soccer-exclusive websites (like LAprepSoccer), soccer-exclusive retails stores (like Club Soccer and Third Coast Soccer), and soccer-exclusive radio shows (like Alan DeRitter's Monday Night Futbol on WGSO). Necessity created this soccer-only culture in the early 1990s, as soccer was locked out by the other three sports.

Soccer in Louisiana was predominantly a men's sport until the 1970s, when youth soccer developed. Female soccer developed in the 1980s, and by the 1990's, women had joined the men in competitive soccer. In 1993, Linda Friedlander and Cindy Perret founded the Greater New Orleans Woman's Soccer League. It would soon fall under the SELASA umbrella. Since that time, it has become known as New Orleans

Co-Ed Soccer (NOSC). This league owes much of its success to the proliferation of girls playground and high school soccer in the late 1970s and 1980s, which is discussed later.

Through ISLANO, the Louisiana Soccer Association was born in 1966. This Louisiana Soccer Association should not be confused with the current LSA, which was officially founded in 1985. Although they share the same name, they do not share the same pedigree. The original Louisiana Soccer Association's first president was Carlos Ross Mitchell Also instrumental to the association's founding was Erik Ruud of Norway. Ruud, you may recall, played with the New Orleans Soccer Club in the 1950s. Its board was predominated by Latinos and European expats. When the Louisiana Soccer Football Association (LSFA), the forerunner to the modern LSA, began in the early 1980s, most of its leaders were American born. The original LSA, however, had non-native leadership and evolved through the 1960s. It was a major organizing force for adult soccer, especially in New Orleans, during the 1970s.

In 1967, the LSA grew and organized rapidly. Elected to be president was Floyd J. Reed; Vice President was Neville Orret; Second Vice President was Dr. Walter Sablinsky. Sablinsky, a Russian historian, spent his undergraduate years playing soccer at the University of California, Berkeley. He became an important leader in Louisiana soccer in the 1960s, helping to coach the Tulane team. (On the next page, Sablinsky is pictured on the top row, third from the right, as the coach of the Tulane club team.)

Back Row: Scott Meyer, Claude Blanc, Buz Fossuni, Tony Verdoni, Randy Miller, Santiago Vilela, Walter Sablinsky, Masciandaro, Keith Yorston, Pedro Haegler, captain, and Jeno Chris Green, Kamel Zakhary. Front Row: Slim Lavassou, Franco Kalozd. Not Pictured are Kelly Moody and Marco Rivera.

1966 *Tulane Jambalaya*

Sablinsky and Mitchell represented Louisiana at the 53rd annual meeting of the U.S. Soccer Football Association in Miami in 1969. Treasurer of the LSA that year was Larry Bishop and Board Member was Alberto Yaguer. Other important figures were George Guiterrez, Louis Ferrand, Nigel Fraser, and Ake Persson.

LSA's original goals were three. They included popularizing youth soccer in Louisiana, spreading the game to parts of Louisiana outside New Orleans, and growing ISLANO so that they could form a professional team out of ISLANO's top players.

The LSA's last goal looked achievable in 1966. Robert Hermann, then president of the North American Soccer League (NASL), made a huge announcement for Louisiana soccer. Hermann said that New Orleans and San Diego would join the NASL in 1967. It looked like the LSA had done it, possibly with the backing of Governor McKeithen who had traveled with the LSU club team to Nicaragua. Truly professional soccer was about to return to Louisiana for the first time in six decades. The home stadium for New Orleans was to be the Superdome (*The Times Picayune*, May 11, 1966).

When the league announced its schedule in 1967, there was a problem. The league's list of teams included only Atlanta, Los Angeles, St. Louis, New York, Chicago, Pittsburg, Baltimore, Philadelphia, California, and Toronto. New Orleans missed the cut somehow! Might there still be hope to bring professional soccer to Louisiana?

In 1968, there was reason to be optimistic. Richard Walsh, president of the North American Soccer League said that one current NASL team would disband. As a result, he said that two cities would receive new pro soccer franchises. He only mentioned three possible candidates: New Orleans, Miami, and Philadelphia. Whatever the reasons, New Orleans did not get a soccer franchise in 1968 either.

If not to pull on the heartstrings of the soccer faithful in New Orleans again, in 1981 Mayor Dutch Morial started drumming up interest in professional soccer in New Orleans. He reached out to several groups hoping they would buy an NASL team and move it to New Orleans.

In August of 1982, Morial's dream looked like it might materialize. The Portland Timbers of the NASL were in dire financial condition. Player salaries rapidly outpaced revenue. The owner of the Timbers, Louisiana-Pacific Corporation, a major building materials manufacturer, said it would "end its ownership of the Portland Timbers and end operations in 30 days if the club is not sold to New Orleans interest" *(The Times Picayune,* August 24, 1982*).*

Officials in New Orleans were giddy. One City Hall employee said, "We have not been actively involved though we are supportive of the idea. We believe that New Orleans, more than most American cities, because of its international background, would be a good place for soccer."

New Orleans, as international as it might have been, did not get the franchise. The Timbers folded in 1982. They would appear again in Portland several years later, and eventually joined the MLS in 2011. Since joining the MLS, the Timbers have averaged attendance above their stadium's capacity over 20,000 each season. New Orleans did not get a professional franchise until 1993, and the MLS still eludes the city.

The LSA's goal of bringing a professional soccer team to Louisiana was not achieved. However, its other two goals, increasing youth participation and spreading the sport to areas throughout the state, were accomplished. The two goals dovetailed perfectly, and as a result of their successful achievement, high school and youth club soccer blossomed. One might even argue that professional soccer's return to Louisiana was a direct product of youth soccer's success in the 1970s and 1980s.

1967-1983: Immigrant High School and Youth Soccer

When members of the original Louisiana Soccer Association set their agenda in the 1960s, they understood that a key component in seeing soccer grow was getting children playing. It was quite simple. How could they expect soccer to take off when very few knew how to play?

Leaders in the Louisiana soccer community repositioned and firmed up community support of the sport in the 1960s, thanks to Hispanic and expat communities, like the Norwegian, Greek, and British. Almost all of these people, however, were adult males. Very few children played the sport, and there were no youth leagues of note. The leaders knew that in order to implant soccer into the culture of Louisiana, getting children playing the game was crucial.

The Jefferson Parish Recreational Department (JPRD) was one of the first, if not the first, youth soccer programs to begin in Louisiana. The official announcement appeared in an inconspicuous two paragraphs in *The Times Picayune*, as seen below.

JPRD Soccer Program Will Begin Saturday

A soccer program for boys 13-year-olds and under will be organized by the Jefferson Parish Recreation Department.

Teams will be organized by Metry Playground, Jefferson Playground, Lakeshore Playground and Airline Park. Starting time for program will be at 2:30 p. m. Saturday.

The Times Picayune, April 8, 1967.

Erik Ruud, the Norwegian who had played soccer in Mexico, played on the New Orleans Soccer Club in the 1950s, and been pivotal in the organization of ISLANO, was one of the first coaches for JPRD. He, along with Bruno Zambon (both pictured below), Manuel Guiterrez, and Dave "Pro" Scheuermann produced a healthy youth soccer league in Jefferson Parish in 1967. Carlos Ross Mitchell, of course, was the biggest force in Louisiana soccer at the time, and had his hand in forming this league.

The first edition of the Louisiana Soccer Association youth state championship was held in 1967 at Jefferson Playground. In the U-15 division, St. Matthias, led by Oscar Bonilla, defeated the JPRD Kickers 2-0. The JPRD Purple Knights captured the U-12 division.

FUTURE STARS — This group of youngsters, 12-year-olds and under, represent the Jefferson Parish Recreation Department's initial soccer program. From left are: Front row, Horace Ferrand, Kenneth Hingle, Ronald Dawson, Bryan Loggins, Mike O'Shello, Lawrence Serena, Mark Lovisa, Keith Champagne; second row, Terry Boudreaux, Dave Scheuermann Jr., Wayne Villemarette, Ray Price, Lee Blakenstein, Leon Casadaban, Hank Hotard, Ray Ranger; third row, coaches Eric Rud, Bruno Zambon, Manuel Gutierrez.

The Times Picayune, June 19, 1967.

A week after JPRD established a league, St. Bernard Parish's Program Director, Ed Heider, announced that his parish also would form a league for boys less than 13 years. The team centered on Our Lady of Lourdes Catholic Church in Violet, about fifteen miles downriver from New Orleans.

Other groups that participated in youth soccer in the 1960s were the YMCA, St. Matthias Elementary School in New Orleans, the Boys Club of Louisiana (1969), and possibly the Plantation Athletic Club (PAC) in Algiers (1963). It is unknown when the PAC first had a soccer team.

While the youth game was developing, Mitchell and Ruud did not forsake the men's soccer league. The league regularly put together all-star teams from ISLANO. The German Consulate sponsored one large game. The New Orleans all-stars accepted the challenge from a German Navy training ship, *Deutchsland*. The homeboys won, 5-1.

The Times Picayune, May 20, 1967

Later that year, the all-stars formed again to play the Yucatan All-Stars from the Yucatan League in Mexico. No score was reported, indicating a probable win for the Mexicans. Noticeable from the picture and roster below is just how Hispanic the ISLANO had become by 1967. Every single player on the roster had a Hispanic name. The youth players, however, were predominantly Euro-American.

MEET YUCATAN TEAM TODAY—The New Orleans Soccer League All-Stars will play the Yucatan, Mexico, All-Star team Sunday at Jefferson Playground at 3 p.m. Members of the New Orleans team, from left, are: Front row, Juan Carlos Mesorio, Roberto Zelaya, Karl G. Munoz, Carlos Doubleday, Robert Castillo, Gustavo Coto; second row, coach Alcides Salcedo, Edwin Ingestroza, Poy Reynaud, Louis Hernandez, Dino Castaneda, Manuel Eguigure, Jose Pignataro; back row, Joaquin Inestroza, Jorge A. Phillips, Carlos Vides, Rodolfo Jese Mesoria, Jesus Coto, Juan Coto and goal tender Manuel "Chino" Cordova.

The Times Picayune, October 10, 1967

1968 was a pivotal year in the history of soccer. It was in 1968 that interscholastic soccer received the organization required to make it self-sustaining. There were already several schools that had teams: Holy Cross (1905), Fortier (1954), Marjorie Walter (1967), Prytania Private School (1967). However, leadership was needed. Carlos Ross Mitchell,

Pro Scheuermann, and most importantly, Brother Alphonse "Al" LeBlanc provided that much-needed leadership.

The Louisiana Soccer Association, sometimes referred to as the Louisiana Soccer Football Association reached out beyond state lines as well. As already mentioned, Dr. Sablinsky and Mitchell were involved in the United States Soccer Football Association. Proof of this and evidence of the talent in Louisiana was the inclusion of two Louisiana players at a national training camp. Steven Ingles and Ricky Mayeaux were chosen to represent the state in St. Louis. In St. Louis, they trained with the U.S. Olympic Committee, the precursor to the Olympic Development Program (ODP). In 1970, Jeff Diemont of the Olympia Club and Horace Ferrand of Fortier High were chosen to represent Louisiana at a similar camp.

The Louisiana Soccer Association was very well organized and got things done in the late 1960s. After nearly attracting a major professional franchise to the city in 1968, leaders of the LSA, including Mitchell, Jose Lazo, and Jose Buendia, recognized that the soccer community needed a stadium built for soccer. They decided that City Park in New Orleans was the best locale.

In conjunction with the City Park Board of Commissioners, the City Park Soccer Football Committee was formed. On September 7, 1969, the field was completed. Mayoral candidate Moon Landrieu cut the ribbon and announced, "With a great deal of luck and with the cooperation of the Highway Department, we have not only a nice field, but a nice clubhouse…(Soccer will be used) as a means of furthering our relations with Latin America" (*The Times Picayune*, September 8, 1969). Landrieu astutely understood the political import of soccer to Latin American nations. Would the city and the state be able to take advantage of it?

In 1968, Brother Al, while at Archbishop Rummel High, organized the first known interscholastic soccer league in Louisiana. There were only four teams: Rummel's 9th grade team, the Jefferson Saints, Our Lady of Lourdes in Violet, and the Costa Rica Juniors.

Favorites to Win Junior Soccer Crown

JPRD'S SAINTS—The Jefferson Parish Recreation Department's Saints are pre-season favorites to win the Louisiana Junior Soccer League. Members of the team are, from left: Front row—Hank Hofard, Mark Lovisa, Jeff Diemont, Eric Gossieaux, Juan Hernandez and Terry Boudreaux. Back row—Leon Casaban, Gus Murillo, Frank Lovisa, coach Bruno Zambon, Dennis Zambon, Ray Ranger and Dave Scheuermann Jr. The league's team will play on Saturdays at Jefferson Playground.

The Times Picayune, January 18, 1968.

The mishmash of high school teams, club teams, and playground teams may seem confusing to contemporary high school soccer fans. However, as with the start of many sports, and many human organizations, rules are loose in the beginning. The longer a group survives, the more likely the group will desire to gain a stronger control over things within its purview. The results of this desire are more rigid rules and structures. As high school soccer grew, the power structure became better organized, and club teams were excluded.

It should be noted again that Holy Cross High School already fielded a team, but did not join this original interscholastic league. Though we recognize Rummel as winning the first interscholastic soccer championship, the team Holy Cross fielded that year was without question the best high school team in the state in 1968. In the Spring of that year, Holy Cross traveled to St. Louis, the birthplace of American high school soccer. There, in the Midwest Junior Cup (today, the James P. McGuire Cup), the Latin Tigers of Holy Cross lost to eventual national champion, St. Phillip Neri, 0-7. St. Phillip Neri, like some of the earliest soccer teams in New Orleans, was a team associated with a Catholic parish or neighborhood, not a school.

1969 saw a further consolidation of the Louisiana Soccer Association. Among those elected were Auguston Cristales (President), Alfred Robles and Fred King of Tulane (Vice Presidents), Bruno Zambon (Treasurer), Dr. Walter Sablinsky (Secretary). Jeanne Del Castillo was appointed as the public relations director; Dave "Pro" Scheuermann as the Junior Commissioner; Carlos Mitchell as the State Development Director. Mitchell was Louisiana's *avant-garde*, recognizing that soccer needed statewide development. He helped make the dream reality.

Vice President Fred King was the captain of the Tulane soccer club. King became coach of the boys team and later, the girls team at Tulane, coaching for a total of twenty years. College soccer had not changed much in the 1970s. From 1966 to 1971, Tulane won the Gulf Coast Soccer League five times. By 1975, Tulane was making big

Southeastern Conference (SEC) news. The Green Wave traveled to face the Rambling Wreck of Georgia Tech in the Finals of the SEC Soccer Classic, held in Atlanta. Tulane walked away as winners, perhaps representing the only SEC soccer champion from Louisiana.

Things for Tulane soccer, however, were not always so grand. To get an idea of how low on the totem pole soccer's place was, King gives us this vivid description in 1962. "Although the Soccer Team enjoys its identity as an athletic club, its lack of funds forces the members to pay for equipment and traveling experiences from their own pockets. In addition, the club must often scrounge or wait for a field, rating a mere third place behind both intramural and fraternity endeavors" (*Tulane Jambalaya*, 1961*).*

1971 Tulane Jambalaya

The University of New Orleans (UNO) began its men's soccer program during this period. The program, started in 1976 under legendary Coach Gerald "Gerry" Mueller, was Louisiana's first men's varsity program. It lasted eleven years, closing in 1986. UNO continues to have a men's club soccer program today, however.

The Olympia Soccer Club, seen in the photograph below, a collection of mostly first generation Honduran American teenagers, won the Junior Cup the next season. The championship included a trophy, but more importantly, the opportunity to represent the state in the Midwest Junior Cup. Again, Louisiana's opponent was St. Phillip of Neri. The two teams played in May at Jefferson Playground. Again, the St. Louis squad triumphed over Louisiana.

SOCCER STYLE—Olympic Soccer Club of New Orleans won the junior cup championship of Louisiana. On the team were, from left, coach Guillermo Solis, Danilo Galindo, Michael Harmon, Maximo Harman, co-captain, Arturo Mejia, Jorge Barrera, Rodolfo Martinez, Mauricio Aguia, Oscar Tabora, Plutarco Trigueros and Carlos R. Mitchell, Louisiana junior commissioner.

The Times Picayune, May 11, 1969.

In 1969, several New Orleans schools formed the Greater New Orleans Interscholastic Soccer Football League (GNOISFL). This league became the New Orleans Interscholastic Soccer League (NOISL), which existed until the end of the 1982 season. The GNOISFL expanded from seven teams in 1968 to ten in 1971 to twelve in 1972. By 1972, there were three division. Division I included Holy Cross, Holy Redeemer Lacombe, Fortier, and Redemptorist NOLA. Division II included Rummel, Country

Day, East Jefferson, and St. Martin's. Division III members were Shaw, Marjorie Walters, Bonnabel, and Warren Easton.

The youth club scene developed in the 1970s. In New Orleans, interscholastic soccer preceded club soccer. However, in much of the state, it was the other way around. Lafreniere Soccer Club in Metairie, for instance, started in 1974. Led through the years by Roy Horos (*The Times Picayune*, July 1, 2007), it dominated club soccer for a good while. Its existence helped feed New Orleans Metro high schools with top players, allowing the area almost to have a monopoly on the early state championships. Founded in 1976, SUNS, the precursor to the Carrollton Soccer Association, also was a pipeline of talent in the New Orleans region.

Specialized soccer clubs had a negative side effect for inner-city soccer and playground soccer. City and parish-based soccer programs, programs like JPRD and the New Orleans Recreational Department (NORD), felt the brunt of this unintended downside. JPRD and NORD both had thriving soccer leagues in the 1970s. When specialized clubs for soccer opened, they drew much of the wealth of talent and funds from the city leagues. As a result, soccer began its move from an urban, immigrant sport to a suburban, predominantly Euro American youth sport.

The 1970s was a decade of near exponential growth for youth soccer in Louisiana, reflecting a national trend. In 1967, about 100,000 Americans played soccer (Bruce Chadwick, "Soccer – Loved and Ignored"). By 1980, that number was nearly one million. By the year 2000, the number topped three million. Since then, the number has remained relatively static, with a slight dip. Some have said that American youth soccer membership has peaked and stabilized.

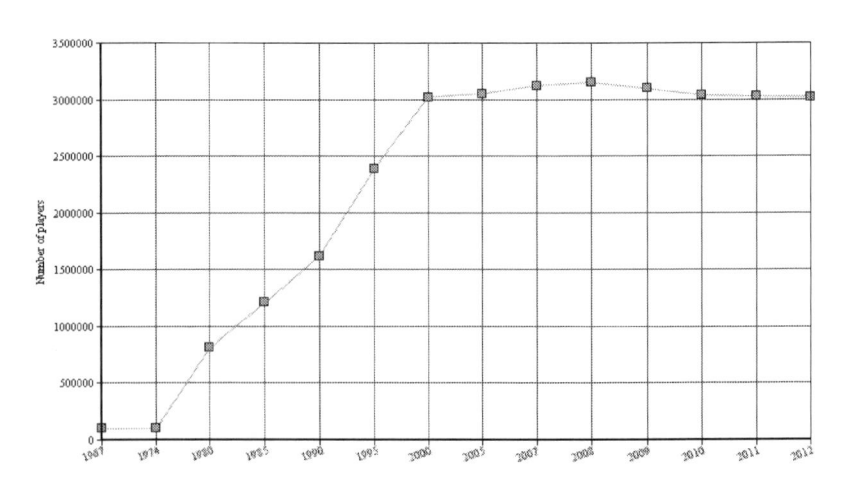

Registered U.S. youth soccer participation

What caused this tremendous growth? Speculative answers range the gambit. Some say it was soccer's appeal to the suburban mom. Soccer was a refined sport that evoked images of Europe. It was also hailed as a safe sport, where injury was rare. Perhaps it was the ease with which the game could be played: no fancy equipment needed, just a ball and some goals. Speculatively, perhaps it was related to the end of segregation in the 1950s. Very few African Americans played soccer; fewer excelled. For some, soccer could have been a subconscious way parents could provide a sport for their child in which there was a small likelihood that their child would compete against African Americans. Perhaps the simplest answer, though, is the most true: soccer is fun. All kids needed was exposure and the game took off.

Louisiana soccer became a pan-Louisiana game in the 1970s. Whereas interscholastic soccer came before club soccer in New Orleans, club soccer predated interscholastic soccer in the rest of the state. The Baton Rouge Soccer Association, for instance, organized in 1975. This club became the main feeder program for the dominant Baton Rouge area high school teams 10-15 years later, namely Catholic High in boys soccer and Baton Rouge High on the girls side.

The Slidell Youth Soccer Club's (SYSC) formation in 1976 was intimately connected to the proud high school programs at Slidell, Pope John Paul II, and Northshore, for both boys and girls, in the late 1980s and early 1990s. The Slidell dominance of both boys and girls high school soccer in those years remains unparalleled by any other community, even New Orleans, in the state.

Soccer came to Lafayette in 1978, and a premier program started there under the banner of the Cajun Soccer Club in 1984. Not surprisingly, 10-15 years later, Lafayette, Acadiana and Episcopal School of Acadiana fielded some of the best teams in Louisiana high school soccer history.

Soccer found its way to Monroe in 1980 with the Northeast Louisiana Soccer Association (NELSA), which produced talent for West Monroe, Ruston, Neville, and St. Frederick. Although none of these schools has won state, they have each produced solid teams, including one state finalist: Neville in 2003.

Caddo Bossier Soccer Association (CABOSA), Houma Terrebonne Soccer Association, and South Tangipahoa Youth Soccer Association (STYSA) began in the 1980s, helping to establish soccer in Shreveport, Houma, and Hammond, respectively. Shreveport-Bossier high schools such as Captain Shreve, Caddo Magnet, Loyola, and Parkway benefitted greatly from CABOSA. In Houma and Thibodaux, Vandebilt Catholic, Central Lafourche, E.D. White, and South Terrebonne have been the beneficiaries of the HTSA and the Blackhawks program. In Hammond, St. Thomas Aquinas, winner of the 2008 state title, has been the primary beneficiary of STYSA.

Carlos Ross Mitchell was instrumental in forming some of these clubs and for running the original Louisiana Soccer Association. He died in 1981, a tremendous blow to the game. His contributions have largely gone unnoted, as he is not enshrined in any sports halls of fame. The LSA disbanded when he died. When it returned in 1985 as an entirely new entity, the Louisiana soccer scene was drastically different.

The early years of youth soccer in Louisiana, 1967 to 1983, saw a dramatic increase in participation. When the period began, almost no children in Louisiana played in organized leagues. By the end of the period, thousands did. Many of the players were American and came from Euro-American backgrounds. However, the best of the players were foreign born or second generation Americans. That social dynamic changed in 1984.

1984: Jesuit's Win Over Warren Easton: The Big Picture

On March 17, 1984, Warren Easton and Jesuit faced each other in Pan American Stadium for the Louisiana Interscholastic Soccer Association's state championship. It was a rematch of the 1983 championship, which saw Warren Easton come away with a 1-0 double overtime win. This 1984 game, however, was bigger than just a state championship. It was a turning point in Louisiana soccer. It marked the end of immigrant dominance of the sport and the rise of soccer as the All American suburban sport.

Hispanic Americans dominated early youth soccer. The Olympia Honduras youth squad won three state championships in a row from 1969 to 1971. When Olympia was no longer allowed to compete in interscholastic soccer, Bonnabel, with its significant Hispanic student body, took the reigns. The biggest name in high school soccer in the late 1970s, though, became Warren Easton.

Warren Easton once boasted quite a tradition, academically and athletically. High school football in New Orleans began when Easton played a group from Tulane in 1896. Numerous doctors, lawyers, generals, and a New Orleans mayor graduated from the school.

Beginning in 1978, Warren Easton began the greatest seven-year run in Louisiana boys high school soccer history. Seven trips to the semifinals. Six trips to the finals. Five championships. Four championships in a row. Other boys programs have approached that greatness, but none has yet to equal the greatness of the Warren Easton reign of the late 70s and early 80s.

Fast forward to 2005. Warren Easton's soccer team captured their district crown, although that district was weak. They advanced to the second round of the playoffs. In the Regionals round, Caddo Magnet of Shreveport dominated the Eagles, 8-0.

That 8-0 loss would be the last game in Warren Easton soccer history. Katrina roared ashore six months later, leaving a devastating wake. Warren Easton remained closed for the entire 2005-2006 school year. When the school reopened, the soccer program did not reopen with it. The floodwaters might have been the death knell in that storied program, but the program was dying years before Katrina came ashore.

Today, eight years after that trip to the 2005 playoffs, soccer remains dead at Warren Easton. There are no indications that the school will field a team next season either. So just what happened at Warren Easton? And what does Warren Easton's demise in soccer tell us about soccer in a broad sense?

Looking back, soccer owes at least part of its rise at Warren Easton to the integration of the schools. The 1954 Supreme Court ruling, Brown vs. Board of Education, of course, required integration. New Orleans delayed implementing that decision until 1960, and even then it was done at a snail's pace. Racial riots were a problem throughout the States in those years, and New Orleans' slow pace for change pushed the integration of Warren Easton back all the way to August 30, 1967, a year before high school soccer in Louisiana was founded. The Times Picayune, in typical Times Picayune fashion bragged about the city's successful integration. "New Orleans systems resumed classes without a hint of racial disturbances which greeted last year's school opening in St. Bernard and Plaquemines."

Before 1967, Warren Easton was an all-white school None of the names listed in that year's yearbook are Hispanic. Were Hispanics allowed into white Orleans Parish Schools before the courts mandated integration? Having a Hispanic or Spanish name in New Orleans did not carry the baggage it might have at the same time in other American cities due to that long history of Hispanic influence in New Orleans. Nonetheless, Warren East appeared to have had few, if any, Hispanic immigrant students before integration.

Integration and a changing neighborhood demographic changed that in the 1970s. Many of these new students were first generation children of workers who had come from Honduras. This international influx led to New Orleans having the nation's densest population of Honduran Americans. By numeric alone, New Orleans has the sixth largest Honduran American population. In addition to changing the look of the neighborhood, these students transformed Warren Easton into a soccer powerhouse.

Hondurans did not initially move to a concentrated area in New Orleans, but Mid-City was an attractive spot for many. Houses were newer and cheaper than in many of the other areas of the city during the 1950s. By the 1970s, Warren Easton had a significant Honduran student population. The soccer-loving population in Warren Easton's school district received boosts in the 1960s and 1980s with the large Cuban and Vietnamese migrations, respectively, to New Orleans. However, the

Vietnamese did not make their presence known on the soccer team until 1986.

By the 1980s, the school zone from which Warren Easton drew its students was international, perhaps more so than any other district in Orleans Parish. On March 12, 1985, the Times Picayune did an article on soccer in Mid-City. The writer mentions daily games on the neutral ground of Jeff Davis. Teams were divided by nationalities, and several of the people interviewed were students at Warren Easton.

Louisiana high school soccer was in its early years in the 1970s when Warren Easton first fielded a team. Under Coach Donald Naylor, Warren Easton ascended to the top very quickly. Most of the players were Hispanic. Some notables included Elvin Garcia and Hugo Martinez. Easton would win titles in the New Orleans Interscholastic Soccer League in 1978, 1979, 1980, and 1981. A truly statewide high school soccer organization, the Louisiana Interscholastic Soccer League (LISA) was organized after the last New Orleans International Soccer League (NOISL) championship in 1981.

Easton would played in two of the first three LISA championships. Both championships pitted the Eagales against Mid-City rival, Jesuit. The teams traded wins, with Jesuit taking the second title in 1984. That loss portended a changing of the guard. Easton was on the way out while Jesuit was establishing itself as the program not only of Mid-City and New Orleans but also of the entire state.

What exactly happened to start the decline? Perhaps it was Coach Naylor's departure. Perhaps the administration at Warren Easton was unsupportive. Perhaps the talent pool dried up as many Honduran families moved to Kenner.

Or perhaps it was a combination of all of these factors with the most important factor of them all: the burgeoning soccer culture in white middle and upper class New Orleans, the pool from which most Jesuit students come. As soccer clubs at Lafreniere and Carrollton grew in the 1970s and 80s, the soccer talent stock at predominantly white schools like Jesuit, Country Day, and De La Salle greatly increased. Fed by these soccer clubs, these private schools commenced a domination of the the sport that exists to this day. On a larger level, Louisiana and American soccer was undergoing a socio-cultural change. This trend was less defined at Slidell High, which won four titles in the 1980s, thanks largely to a well-run club program that began there in the 1970s. Most of Slidell's male talent was European American, although Slidell's top talent during this period was Latino American.

Warren Easton quickly became a less diverse school in the late 1980s. Easton became predominantly an African American school as a result of middle class flight to the suburbs during this and previous decades. Soccer within the New Orleans African American community has never been very popular. Several well-intentioned, but poorly funded campaigns existed in the 1990s and 2000s to bring soccer to the inner-city to introduce the game to the African American community. These efforts as of today have not produced profound results. One result of Warren Easton's African American homogenization was a decrease in its soccer program's success.

1984 was the last year Warren Easton reached the state championship. Since 1984, Jesuit has been to seventeen state championship games, winning eleven.

The story of Warren Easton soccer is one of meteoric climb and descent nearly as grand. A stream of international, national, and metropolitan cultural forces affected the program. Warren Easton's soccer program has largely been forgotten, stowed away in old newspaper archives, but its place among the all-time greatest Louisiana high school soccer programs is already cemented.

Likewise, Jesuit's state championship in 1984 served as a harbinger of things to come. No longer would first and second-generation immigrants dominate the youth soccer scene. Youth soccer became, for the most part, a sport for those who could afford to spend large amounts of money on professional coaching and weekends on the road traveling to out-of-state soccer tournaments [A July 6, 1982 article by *The Times Picayune*'s Kerry Luft was the first to notice the changing demographic of youth soccer.].

1985-2013: The All American Sport

Jesuit's triumph in 1984 signaled a new era in Louisiana soccer, the age of All American soccer. It was a national trend, as club and high school soccer became predominately a wealthy, suburban sport. First and second generation immigrants still played the sport, but most could not keep up with the well-oiled machines that money and stability provided in the maturing youth soccer clubs. The individual talent of some immigrant children fell behind the team talent of the All American soccer teams.

For decades, soccer had been an immigrant sport in Louisiana and a way for immigrant communities to maintain their own culture and practice rituals associated with that culture. As soccer entered the 1980s, ironically, some saw the game as just the opposite. Soccer could be a way to push immigrant students into the sea of American culture. "These kids [Hispanic and Vietnamese] are getting into the mainstream of the soccer program. It's a way for them to become more assimilated. It's very positive," said Lou Zenowich, president of the Louisiana Interscholastic Soccer Association in 1983 (T.P. 3/18/1983).

The irony come from the fact that from the 1850s to the 1960s, and in many ways, all the way to the present, foreign born soccer players used soccer as a way of maintaining their own ethnic identities. The first German and Irish soccer players in Louisiana used the game to maintain ties to their native culture. Later, players from Honduras joined Honduran clubs in New Orleans. They played against other Hispanic teams. They spoke Spanish on the field. They ate the traditional foods of their native lands after the game. Groups from Honduras, Guatemala, and other nations gathered to watch players from their respective countries play soccer on Scout Island or Pan American Stadium in City Park. This scene repeats itself today. Soccer is very much a device of cultural preservation in the Latino community. In some ways, it is today a cultural preservative greater than the Catholic Church, which historically has been the community's greatest point of meeting.

Indeed, as a show of the strong cultural significance soccer plays in the Latino community of New Orleans, several professional from Central America have traveled to the city in recent years. In 2011, Motagua of Tegucigalpa, Honduras, the birth city of Carlos Ross Mitchell, beat fellow Honduran squad, Olimpia, 3-2 at Tad Gormley before 8,000. Having seen that success, an out-of-state promoter set up a game a month later between Motagua and Mexico City based Club America. Tropical Storm Lee came ashore the day of the game, dumping up to ten inches of rain in the area. Still, an estimated crowd of 2,500 came out to watch the Mexican squad triumph.

For the first time in the 1980s, both American and immigrant cultures embrace soccer as their own. However, there is a deep divide in immigrant soccer and American soccer in Louisiana. Rarely are Euro-American players found in the stands or on the fields of ISLANO. There are exceptions of excellent Euro-American players in ISLANO, of course, but they are just that. This ethnic division amongst soccer fans goes back decades, and the division is a large reason why professional soccer has not succeeded in Louisiana. The only way New Orleans or Louisiana will ever get an MLS franchise is if the Latino and Euro-American soccer communities come together. However, the two communities are still a considerable distance apart.

When the 1990s began professional soccer was last seen, yet not remembered, in Louisiana in 1908. The state skirted with the possibility of bringing in teams in 1967 and again in 1982, but both times, New Orleans did not prove worthy. That changed in 1993 when Donnie Pate brought the Riverboat Gamblers to New Orleans.

Initially, the Gamblers played their games at Pan American. Crowds in the first years were large. It was not unusual to have 3,000 in attendance. The team eventually moved to Tad Gormley Stadium.

It was at Tad Gormley Stadium in 1996 that the second largest crowd ever to watch a soccer game in Louisiana gathered. They came to see the Gamblers face the U-23 U.S. Men's National Team. Before a raucous crowd 11,876 Hispanic and Euro-American fans, the Gamblers eked out a 1-1 draw.

A year later, the Gamblers drew over 6,000 for a U.S. Open Cup game against the MLS Dallas Burn. Former Gamblers player Jason Kreis scored the winning goal for Dallas.

The following year, New Orleans was selected to host the two semifinal games of the U.S. Open Cup. In truth, it was an audition before the MLS to determine if the city was ready to have an MLS franchise. By this point, Rob Couhig, owner of the New Orleans Zephyrs AAA baseball team, also owned the soccer franchise. Storm coach Daryl Shore said, "Maybe this is a chance to see if we can get an MLS team here" (*The Times Picayune*, August 5, 1998)." The 6,154 fans who watched must not have impressed the MLS staff. Only one time since has an MLS team traveled to play in Louisiana.

Lafayette and Baton Rouge also claimed professional teams in 1997. The Lafayette Swampcats and the Baton Rouge Bombers achieved success through the Eastern Indoor Soccer League. The Swampcats won the league twice, and the Bombers finished second in the league in 1997. Both teams' rosters were filled with locals, often former high school and club stars, but ultimately, that league failed after just two seasons.

While the crowds that MLS teams playing exhibitions in New Orleans were large, the largest crowd ever to watch a soccer game in Louisiana gathered in 2003. More than 15,000 spectators came and saw the U.S. Women's National Team beat the Brazilian national squad 1-0. That is correct: the largest soccer crowd in Louisiana history watched a women's game. That may surprise some, but it should not. The 1999 Women's World Cup Final had the second largest television audience in American soccer history, and one of the largest non-football television audiences in American sports history.

The female soccer craze, however, only happened because of a national phenomenon in the 1970s. Girls started playing soccer. It happened in Louisiana as well at this time.

Women at Newcomb College (Tulane) began playing soccer in 1937. There was no league and it was recreational in nature, without much competition. Forty years later, in 1976, that changed. Finally, the Tulane women fielded a club team that played other women's teams in the region. Since its founding in 1976, Tulane has had a competitive women's club soccer team every year to the present. Moreover, the success of the women's club team helped give rise to the varsity women's program at Tulane in 1996.

By 1981, there was a women's soccer league in New Orleans. Little is known about this league, but the two top teams were the Tulane women and the Hellenic Glory, sister team to the Greek-American Soccer Club of New Orleans. Led by team MVP, Mary Whitlow, the Green Wave finished 10-1-1 in 1981. Tulane's one loss was in the championship game to the undefeated Hellenic Glory.

The first girls' soccer clubs began in the mid-1970s at Plantation Athletic Club (PAC) and SUNS, the forerunner to the Carrollton Soccer Association. Shortly after, those two clubs, and a Latino side named Vita, were joined by Lafreniere Soccer Club, Slidell Youth Soccer Club, and the Baton Rouge Soccer Association. In the early years of girls' high school soccer, these clubs helped build strong programs at Slidell High, Northshore High, Country Day, Newman, and Baton Rouge High.

Although girls played soccer in Louisiana all the way back in the 1920s and 1930s, organized high school ball did not start for girls until 1977. Harold Bretz, coach for the O. Perry Walker Chargerettes of Algiers formed this league. It was extremely rudimentary. There were four teams: O.P. Walker, Country Day, St. Martin's, the eventual champion, and runner-up McGehee. Each team played just three games.

Simple as it was, the 1977 high school league brought attention to girls' soccer. Following a two-year hiatus, girls' high school soccer returned, this time with an eight-team league. Growth was not instantaneous: there were only fourteen teams in the league five years later. The only non-New Orleans team was Baton Rouge High. The inclusion of a non-New Orleans team and the spread of the sport throughout Louisiana through the club game caused the rapid expansion of the girls' high school game. By 1990, there were teams throughout Louisiana, from Baton Rouge to Lafayette to Lake Charles to Shreveport. The game had become so popular by 1995 that the league split into two divisions based on enrollment size. The league split into three divisions in 2001 to accommodate even more teams.

This era of Louisiana girls soccer mirrored that of the rest of American girls soccer. In 1976, the year before O.P. Walker fielded a team, there were approximately 10,000 female high school players in the nation. By 1980, when local girls soccer really began to expand, there were 40,000 players nationally.

An important moment for the high school game came in 1986. It was that year that the sport finally got recognition from the Louisiana High School Athletic Association (LHSAA). It was a long time coming and long overdue, at least for the well organized boys' league. One of the important figures in the movement to achieve LHSAA status was Teddy Cotonio, the late former principle of Newman.

Club soccer developed rapidly in the mid-1980s. The timeline in the front of the book shows just how many club soccer teams were added during this period. The pan-Louisiana growth of the game at the club and playground level laid the foundation for many high school soccer programs that began in the late 1990s and early 2000s. This formation was different from what we saw in New Orleans, where high school soccer predated the club game.

One of the major stories in club soccer history includes the 1991 United Jaguars of Baton Rouge. The Jags were the first Louisiana youth team to play for a national soccer championship. Mandeville's Jason Kreis, future MLS MVP, U.S. National Team player, and Real Salt Lake coach, returned to his childhood home of Omaha, Nebraska. There the team faced North Huntington Beach of California, a team that had on its roster two future U.S. National Team players. The team from Baton Rouge, missing its starting goalkeeper, was outmatched from the beginning. The Jags lost 1-7. However, that team set a standard only one other Louisiana team [the Lafreniere Gamblers '78 boys in 1995] before or since has matched

Another very important development for the club game that had a profound impact on the high school game as well was the introduction of professional soccer coaches in New Orleans club teams. The first came in 1990, Franz Van Balkom, a legendary coach who coached a couple national teams, including Hong Kong, and in Japan's premier professional division. He founded FVB near the UNO campus. FVB became the New Orleans Soccer Academy (NOSA) in 1994, led by Marc Nichols.

Also noteworthy was the hiring of Mike Jeffries at Lafreniere in 1993. The move was likely in response to the FVB soccer academy formed in New Orleans three years earlier. Jeffries was a Hermann Award winner for top collegiate player in the nation in 1983 and made several appearances with the U.S. National Team. He was one of the first professional coaches in youth soccer in Louisiana and introduced small-sided soccer to the state. In small-sided soccer, less than eleven players play against each other in shortened field. The goal is to allow each player more touches on the ball. Jeffries and Van Balkom's time in Louisiana greatly elevated the level of play in New Orleans and in the rest of the state, as other clubs tried to stay even.

On the college scene, the UNO men's team disbanded in the mid-1980s. Women's club teams continued to exist throughout the state's colleges. The 1990s, however, saw many of those programs become varsity programs. The cause was Title IX.

Congress passed Title IX in 1972. The law was intended to prevent gender discrimination on college campuses. Though long in the making, the effects of Title IX did not affect women's soccer in Louisiana until the mid-1990s. The new law forced athletic programs to offer an equal opportunity for female athletes as males. In order for the programs to keep competitive football teams stocked with the NCAA limit of scholarship athletes, the universities chose to form women's programs. Women's soccer saw a boom through the 1990s, when varsity programs began at LSU, Tulane, ULL, ULM, McNeese State, and SLU among others.

While Title IX was the catalyst for collegiate women's varsity soccer programs in the state, Title IX is said by many to be the reason Louisiana lacks a major varsity level men's soccer program. As a result, some proponents of men's college soccer in Louisiana resent Title IX, as they see the law as an impediment for men's varsity level teams. Rumors about LSU starting a men's program are annually passed around, often triggering resentment of Title IX. The line of reason that follows is that in order for a college to start a men's soccer program, the college would have to start a new women's sport in order to keep the scholarship gender ratio equal. College athletic departments, not wanting to entail the high costs of starting two programs, refuse to do it.

Such reasoning, however, misses the bigger picture, a picture that shows how collegiate sports fell from providing a service to students for achieving athletic excellence, as in the Greek gymnasium model, to purely that of a business. Title IX is less to blame for the lack of men's soccer than the culture that exists in athletic departments in Louisiana. The problem came when athletic departments became independent organizations that carried the university's name, but not the university's *ethos*. The transformation of athletic departments from branches of the universities to quasi-independent businesses began in the 1960s, largely as a product of television sports contracts. What seems to determine if a school starts a sports program today is not if the program will benefit the students of the university. Does the law mandate the sport? and Will the sport generate a profit? are the two crucial questions athletic departments ask today.

At LSU, the administration does not request that the athletic department provide for its students and the soccer players of Louisiana a varsity men's program, in my opinion, because the athletic department does not want to pay to field another team. The university administration does not stand up for soccer because the athletic department keeps a steady stream of millions of dollars flowing to the university (currently about $7 million each year).

Considering that Louisiana has produced three of the top collegiate men's players in America in the last decade, signifying its vibrant youth soccer development, and the flagship university's duty to bring out excellence in the talented youth of the state, the decades-long refusal of the athletic department to field a varsity level men's program, and the university's acquiescence, should be frowned upon. In short, it is long overdue that the flagship public university of Louisiana field a men's varsity level soccer program.

Another problem that has plagued soccer in Louisiana is a general lack of coverage from the media. Although there have been excellent soccer reporters, soccer has, by and large, been treated as a minor sport by the papers and television stations of Louisiana. LAprepSoccer was born to address this issue. Hoping to improve rankings, increase access to scores and standings, promote sportsmanship, and archive the results of high school soccer, Scott Crawford founded what would become LAprepSoccer.net in the Fall of 1999. The website quickly grew in popularity. Its community has helped organize and rally the soccer community on many occasions.

With the success of the girls game, the continuation of immigrant-based leagues, a continuation of semi-pro soccer in New Orleans with the Jesters, and the healthy club scene, soccer in Louisiana has become a part of the culture of the state. What was once absurd to say – that soccer might surpass baseball or basketball in popularity one day soon – is no longer out of the question. The All American sport of soccer has arrived in Louisiana.

Conclusion

We have traced the rise of soccer through German and Irish immigrant populations in New Orleans during the 1850s. Three decades later, we also saw soccer become a popular sport amongst the elite athletic clubs of New Orleans. By the first decade of the twentieth century, New Orleans had a professional soccer league that sent several players to the top professional soccer leagues of Europe. After that league collapsed, soccer was limited to the Hispanic immigrant and European expat population, along with visiting ships' crew teams, until the 1960s. In the 1960s, youth soccer at the club and high school levels began. Since then, soccer has become one of the most popular sports in Louisiana with nearly 30,000 registered players.

Nonetheless, Louisiana lags behind the national average of youth soccer participants in America. Louisiana makes up 1.46% of America's population. If all things were equal, Louisiana would have around 1.5% of US Youth Soccer's registered players. However, as of 2012, Louisiana had just 27,000 registered players, making up just 0.9% of nationally registered youth players. This gap of 0.6% is statistically significant. The MLS has not made any indications it might expand to Louisiana. All that shows Louisiana is behind the curve in American soccer.

Despite all that, Louisiana has managed to produce one U.S. Men's National Team player in the 1990s and three male Hermann Award winners since 2005 (Jason Garey, Joseph Lapira, and Patrick Mullins). Since 1980, when the Hermann Award shifted away from a St. Louis-centric award, only New York and New Jersey have produced more Hermann Award winners. Even then, neither state has produced a winner since 2003. On the girls side, Louisiana produced a member of the 1996 U.S. Olympic team in Jenny Streiffer Mascaro.

The history of soccer in Louisiana is rich and colorful. Louisiana is one of the first locations in the world where modern soccer existed. Soccer is the state of Louisiana's oldest played team ball sport, older than basketball, baseball, and football. And yet, until this book, soccer was assumed to have started relatively recently in Louisiana. One of the biggest obstacles facing soccer in Louisiana today is bridging the cultural and historical gap between Latino and Euro American soccer communities. An additional obstacle Louisiana soccer must overcome is the lack of a men's varsity soccer program at LSU, Tulane, and UL Lafayette. With club traditions that trace back a hundred years, these schools should begin the process of building men's varsity soccer programs. Soccer will continue to grow in Louisiana this century, but if the Hispanic and Euro American soccer communities grow to be one and LSU and Tulane field varsity men's programs, expect the growth to be phenomenal.

Appendices

Louisiana High School Soccer Boys State Championship Games (1968-2013)[1]

Governing bodies of Louisiana high school soccer:
Interscholastic Junior Soccer League: I.J.S.L. (1967-1968)
Greater New Orleans Interscholastic Soccer Football League: (1968-1971)
New Orleans Interscholastic Soccer League: N.O.I.S.L. (1971-1982)
Louisiana Interscholastic Soccer Association: L.I.S.A. (1982-1986)
Louisiana High School Athletic Association: LHSAA (1986-present)

1967-1968 (Interscholastic Junior Soccer League)
Rummel 2 Jefferson (JPRD) Saints 0 (at Jefferson Playground)

1968-1969 (Greater New Orleans Interscholastic Soccer Football League)
Olympia defeated Holy Cross

1969-1970 (Greater New Orleans Interscholastic Soccer Football League)
Olympia defeated Fortier

1970-1971 (Greater New Orleans Interscholastic Soccer Football League)
Olympia defeated Redemptorist NOLA (Redeemer-Seton)

1971-1972 (New Orleans Interscholastic Soccer League)
Redemptorist NOLA 4 Olympia 1 (at City Park) April 3, 1972

1972-1973 (New Orleans Interscholastic Soccer League)
Champion: Holy Cross (8-0-3)
Runner-Up: Rummel (9-1-2)

1973-1974 (New Orleans Interscholastic Soccer League)
Rummel 2 Bonnabel 1 OT (at Pan American Field) February 16, 1974

1974-1975 (New Orleans Interscholastic Soccer League)
Rummel defeated Bonnabel (at Pan American Stadium) February 22, 1975

---

[1] This list and links to newspaper articles and photographs about the games can be found on the LAprepSoccer forum: http://laprepsoccer.proboards.com/thread/15718/

1975-1976 (New Orleans Interscholastic Soccer League)
Country Day 3 Bonnabel 2 (at Pan American Stadium) February 14, 1976

1976-1977 (New Orleans Interscholastic Soccer League)
De La Salle beat Country Day

1977-1978 (New Orleans Interscholastic Soccer League)
Warren Easton beat Newman (at St. Martin's) February 28, 1978

1978-1979 (New Orleans Interscholastic Soccer League)
Warren Easton 5 Jesuit 1 (at O. Perry Walker Field) February 24, 1979

1979-1980 (New Orleans Interscholastic Soccer League)
Warren Easton beat Newman (OT) (at Pan American Stadium)

1980-1981 (New Orleans Interscholastic Soccer League)
Warren Easton 4 Bonnabel 2 (at Pan American Stadium) February 21, 1981

1981-1982 (New Orleans Interscholastic Soccer League)
De La Salle 4 Shaw 2 (at Pan American Stadium) March 10, 1982

1982-1983 (Louisiana Interscholastic Soccer Association)
Warren Easton 1 Jesuit 0 (2OT) (at Pan American Stadium) March 12, 1983

1983-1984 (Louisiana Interscholastic Soccer Association)
Jesuit 2 Warren Easton 1 (at Pan American Stadium) March 17, 1984

1984-1985 (Louisiana Interscholastic Soccer Association)
Slidell 3 Mandeville 2 (2 OT) (at Pan American Stadium) February 16, 1985

1985-1986 (Louisiana Interscholastic Soccer Association):
Slidell 4 Ben Franklin 1 (at Pan American Stadium) March 20, 1986

1986-1987 (LHSAA):
Jesuit 1 Rummel 0 (at Lupin Field, Newman) March 28, 1987

1987-1988:
Slidell 7 Comeaux 1 (at Episcopal of Baton Rouge) March 26, 1988

1988-1989:

Slidell 2 Northshore 0 (at Slidell High) February 25, 1989

1989-1990:
Div I: Catholic BR 2 De La Salle 1 2OT (at Baton Rouge High) February 24, 1990
Div II: Episcopal School of Acadiana defeated Vandebilt

1990-1991:
Div I: Catholic BR 3 De La Salle 1 (at Westdale Middle School Baton Rouge) February 23, 1991
Div II: Woodlawn 2 Episcopal School of Acadiana 1 (at Woodlawn Baton Rouge)

1991-1992:
Div I: Slidell 4 Catholic BR 1 (at Westdale Middle School Baton Rouge) March 1, 1992
Div II: Vandebilt 4 St. Thomas More 1 (at Comeaux)

1992-1993:
Div I: Catholic BR 2 Slidell 0 (at Slidell High) February 27, 1993
Div II: Newman 2 St. Thomas More 1 (at Lupin Field, Newman) February 20, 1993

1993-1994:
Div I: De La Salle 3 Jesuit 2 (at Roosevelt Mall in N.O. City Park) February 26, 1994
Div II: Bishop Sullivan 1 Vandebilt 0 (at Woodlawn BR) February 19, 1994 (Bishop Sullivan became St. Michael's)

1994-1995:
Div I: Jesuit 3 Catholic BR 2 (at Rebel Field, R.E. Lee) February 25, 1995
Div II: Newman 1 Episcopal School of Acadiana 0 (at Lupin Field, Newman) February 18, 1995

1995-1996:
Div I: Mandeville 2 Jesuit 1 (at Ecole Classique) February 26, 1996
Div II: Loyola 2 Baton Rouge 1 (at Caddo Parish Stadium) February 17, 1996
Div III: Vandebilt 2 Newman 1 (at Terrier Field, Vandebilt) February 17, 1996

1996-1997:
Div I: Acadiana 3 Jesuit 1 (at Pan American Stadium) March 1, 1997
Div II: St. Paul's 2 Baton Rouge 0 (at Rebel Field, R.E. Lee) February 22, 1997
Div III: St. Louis 4 St. Martin's 0 (at St. Martin's) February 22, 1997

1997-1998:
Div I: Acadiana 1 Lafayette 0 (at Mighty Lion Stadium, Lafayette) February 28, 1998
Div II: St. Paul's 2 Baton Rouge 0 (at Rebel Field, R.E. Lee) February 25, 1998
Div III: St. Louis 3 Newman 1 (at St. Louis Catholic) February 28, 1998

1998-1999:
Div I: Jesuit 3 Acadiana 0 (at Zephyr Field, Metairie) February 27, 1999
Div II: Woodlawn BR 5 St. Paul's 1 (OT) (at Hunter Stadium, St. Paul's High) February 24, 1999
Div III: Newman 4 Parkview Baptist 2 (at Lupin Field, Newman) February 27, 1999

1999-2000:
Div I: Brother Martin 3 Jesuit 0 (at Pan American Stadium) February 26, 2000
Div II: St. Paul's 3 Woodlawn BR 2 (OT) (at Woodlawn BR) February 23, 2000
Div III: Parkview Baptist 2 Loyola 1 (OT) (at Caddo Parish Stadium) February 26, 2000

2000-2001:
Div I: Brother Martin 1 Acadiana 0 (at Tad Gormley Stadium) February 28, 2001
Div II: St. Thomas More 3 Parkway 1 (at Independence Stadium) February 21, 2001
Div III: Newman 2 St. Martin's 0 (at Tad Gormley Stadium) March 1, 2001

2001-2002:
Div I: Jesuit 3 Brother Martin 0 (at Tad Gormley Stadium) February 23, 2002
Div II: Vandebilt 2 South Terrebonne 0 (at Terrier Field, Vandebilt) February 23, 2002

Div III: St. Martin's 3 St. Louis 1 (at Tad Gormley Stadium) February 22, 2002

2002-2003:
Div I: Jesuit 2 Lafayette 1 (at Tad Gormley Stadium) March 8, 2003
Div II: Vandebilt 2 Neville 1 (at Terrier Field, Vandebilt) March 6, 2003
Div III: St. Louis 3 St. Thomas Aquinas 0 (at Tad Gormley Stadium) March 7, 2003

2003-2004:
Div I: Lafayette 1 Jesuit 0 (at Tad Gormley Stadium) February 28, 2004
Div II: Ben Franklin 1 Vandebilt 0 (at Terrier Field, Vandebilt) February 28, 2004
Div III: St. Louis 6 St. Martin's 1 (at Tad Gormley Stadium) February 27, 2004

2004-2005:
Div I: Jesuit 3 Lafayette 2 (OT) (at Tad Gormley Stadium) February 26, 2005
Div II: Vandebilt 1 Ben Franklin 0 (at Buddy Marcello Stadium, Vandebilt) February 26, 2005
Div III: Newman 3 St. Martin's 2 (at Tad Gormley Stadium) February 25, 2005

2005-2006:
Div I: Carencro 3 Fontainebleau 1 (at ULL Soccer Complex) March 4, 2006
Div II: Vandebilt 8 East Ascension 0 (at Spartan Stadium, East Ascension) March 4, 2006
Div III: St. Louis 3 Teurlings 0 (at ULL Soccer Complex) March 3, 2006

2006-2007:
Div I: Jesuit 2 St. Paul's 0 (at Independence Stadium) February 24, 2007
Div II: Vandebilt 3 East Ascension 0 (at Spartan Stadium, East Ascension) February 24, 2007
Div III: St. Louis 1 Teurlings 0 (2OT) (at Independence Stadium) February 23, 2007

2007-2008:
Div I: Caddo 2 Woodlawn 1 (at Independence Stadium) February 23, 2008
Div II: Teurlings 1 Vandebilt 1 (Teurlings 4-2 in pks) (at ULL Soccer Complex) February 16, 2008

Div III: St. Thomas Aquinas 1 Newman 0 (at Independence Stadium) February 22, 2008

2008-2009:
Div I: Jesuit 3 Captain Shreve 1 (at Independence Stadium) February 28, 2009
Div II: Teurlings 4 Loyola 1 (at Messmer Stadium, Loyola Shreveport) February 21, 2009
Div III: Newman 2 University 1 (2OT) (at Independence Stadium) February 27, 2009

2009-2010:
Div I: Jesuit 2 Lafayette 1 (at Independence Stadium) February 27, 2010
Div II: St. Louis 2 Vandebilt 1 (at Vandebilt) February 27, 2010
Div III: Newman 2 University 1 (at Independence Stadium) February 26, 2010

2010-2011:
Div I: St. Paul's 2 Jesuit 1 (at Tad Gormley Stadium) February 26, 2011
Div II: St. Louis 1 Vandebilt 0 (at McNeese State University Soccer Complex) February 26, 2011
Div III: Northlake Christian 3 Ben Franklin 0 (at Tad Gormley) February 25, 2011

2011-2012
Div I: Jesuit 3 St. Paul's 2 (at Tad Gormley Stadium) February 25, 2012
Div II: St. Louis 1 Ben Franklin 0 (at Tad Gormley Stadium) February 24, 2012
Div III: Country Day 1 Northlake Christian 0 (at Tad Gormley Stadium) February 25, 2012

2012-2013
Div I: Jesuit 2 St. Paul's 1 (OT) (at Tad Gormley Stadium) February 23, 2013
Div II: St. Louis 3 Beau Chene 0 (at Tad Gormley Stadium) February 23, 2013
Div III: Episcopal BR 2 Newman 1 (OT) (at Tad Gormley Stadium) February 22, 2013

Head coach records in the Louisiana high school boys' soccer championship games

Jason Oertling, St. Louis Catholic: (10-1). Wins: 1997, 1998, 2003, 2004, 2006, 2007, 2010, 2011, 2012, 2013. Loss: 2002.
Gerry Mueller, De La Salle & Newman: (7-2). Wins: 1977, 1982 (DLS); 1993, 1995, 1999, 2001, 2005 (Newman) Losses: 1996, 1998
Hubie Collins, Jesuit: (7-2). Wins: 2003, 2005, 2007, 2009, 2010, 2012, 2013. Losses: 2004, 2011.
Doug Hamilton, Vandebilt Catholic: (6-2). Wins: 1996, 2002, 2003, 2005, 2006, 2007. Losses: 2004, 2008.
Donald Naylor, Warren Easton: (5-1). Wins: 1978, 1979, 1980, 1981, 1983. Loss: 1984.
Seamous Diamond, Slidell High: (4-0). Wins: 1985, 1986, 1988, 1989.
Garry Ortner, Jesuit: (3-4). Wins: 1995, 1999, 2002. Losses: 1994, 1996, 1997, 2000.
Brother Al LeBlanc, Rummel: (3-2). Wins: 1968, 1974, 1975. Losses: 1973, 1987.
Carlos Ross Mitchell, Olympia: (3-1). Wins: 1969, 1970, 1971. Loss: 1972.
Lance Peltier, Teurlings Catholic: (2-2). Wins: 2008, 2009. Losses: 2006, 2007.
Matt Jacques, Newman: (2-2). Wins: 2009, 2010. Losses: 2008, 2013.
Glenn Laviolette, Acadiana: (2-1). Wins: 1997, 1998. Loss: 1999.
Brother Tim Coldwell, St. Paul's: (2-1). Wins: 1998, 2000. Loss: 1999.
Alan DeRitter, Brother Martin: (2-1). Wins: 2000, 2001. Loss: 2002.
Julio Paiz, St. Martin's: (1-4). Win: 2002. Losses: 1997, 2001, 2004, 2005.
Diego Gonzalez, Ben Franklin: (1-2). Win: 2004. Losses: 1986, 2005.
Stavros Savvaides, De La Salle: (1-2). Win: 1994. Losses: 1990, 1991.
Duaine Belfour, Lafayette: (1-2). Win: 2004. Losses: 2003, 2005.
Sean Moser, St. Paul's: (1-2). Win: 2011. Losses: 2012, 2013.
John Cicchino, Catholic BR: (1-1). Win: 1991. Loss: 1992.
Iggy Baggetta, Slidell High: (1-1). Win: 1992. Loss: 1993.
Shelley McMillian, Loyola: (1-1). Win: 1996. Loss: 2000.
Trevor Watkins, St. Paul's: (1-1). Win: 1997. Loss: 2007.
John Cox, St. Thomas Aquinas: (1-1). Win: 2008. Loss: 2003.
Nick Chetta, Northlake Christian: (1-1). Win: 2011. Loss: 2012.
George Lesperance, Jesuit: (1-0). Win: 1984.
Bob Melia, Jesuit: (1-0). Win: 1987.
Kevin Couhig, Catholic BR: (1-0). Win: 1990.
Ed Hardin, Catholic BR: (1-0). Win: 1993.
Scott Fontenot, Bishop Sullivan: (1-0). Win: 1994.
Richard Yeadon, Mandeville: (1-0). Win: 1996.

Eric England, Woodlawn BR: (1-0). Win: 1999.
Craig Winchell, Parkview Baptist: (1-0). Win: 2000.
Willie Davis, St. Thomas More: (1-0). Win: 2001.
Kert Talley, Carencro: (1-0). Win: 2006.
Radi Baltov, Caddo Magnet: (1-0). Win: 2008.
Aris Kyriakides, Country Day: (1-0). Win: 2012.
Chris Stewart, Episcopal BR: (1-0). Win: 2013.
Rueben Ruiz, East Ascension: (0-2). Losses: 2006, 2007.
Chris Mitchell, University: (0-2). Losses: 2009, 2010.
Matt Kelso, Vandebilt Catholic: (0-2). Losses: 2010, 2011.
Bruno Zambon, JPRD Saints: (0-1). Loss: 1968.
Brother Phillip Babineaux, Holy Cross: (0-1). Loss: 1970.
Brother Louis Coe, Holy Cross: (0-1). Loss: 1972.
Ralph Bergeron, Jesuit: (0-1). Loss: 1979.
Mike Conway, Jesuit: (0-1). Loss: 1983.
Al Lasher, Northshore: (0-1). Loss: 1989.
John Telford, Vandebilt: (0-1). Loss: 1994.
David Chaney, Episcopal School of Acadiana (0-1). Loss: 1995.
John Knighten, Baton Rouge High: (0-1). Loss: 1997.
Jim Simon, Lafayette High: (0-1). Loss: 1998.
Jake Vezinat, Baton Rouge High: (0-1). Loss: 1998.
John Green, Parkview Baptist: (0-1). Loss: 1999.
Joe Gallucci, Parkway: (0-1). Loss: 2001.
Mark Hopkins, Acadiana: (0-1). Loss: 2001.
Randy Boquet, South Terrebonne: (0-1). Loss: 2002.
Stuart Keys, Neville: (0-1). Loss: 2003.
Budd Ditchendorf, Fontainebleau: (0-1). Loss: 2006.
Matt Smith, Captain Shreve: (0-1). Loss: 2009.
Stephen Slack, Loyola: (0-1). Loss: 2009.
Grant Guthrie, Ben Franklin: (0-1). Loss: 2011.
Jose Ferrand, Ben Franklin: (0-1). Loss: 2012.
Chad Vidrine, Beau Chene: (0-1). Loss: 2013.

Louisiana High Schools Girls State Championships (1977-2013)

1977
Champion: St. Martin's
Runner-Up: McGehee

1977-1978: unknown

1978-1979: unknown

1979-1980 New Orleans Interscholastic Soccer League State Championship
Country Day 1 Warren Easton 0 (at Pan American Stadium) February 16, 1980

1980-1981 New Orleans Interscholastic Soccer League State Championship
Country Day 3 Bonnabel 2 (at Pan American Stadium) February 21, 1981

1981-1982 New Orleans Interscholastic Soccer Association State Championship
unknown (at Pan American Stadium)

1982-1983 Louisiana Interscholastic Soccer Association State Championship
Slidell defeated Country Day (at Pan American Stadium) March 5, 1983

1983-1984 Louisiana Interscholastic Soccer Association State Championship
Northshore 3 Slidell 2 (at Pan American Stadium) March 17, 1984

1984-1985 Louisiana Interscholastic Soccer Association State Championship
Slidell 1 Northshore 0 (at Pan American Stadium) February 16, 1985

1985-1986 Louisiana Interscholastic Soccer Association State Championship
Northshore 1 Slidell 0 (at Pan American Stadium) March 15, 1986

1986-1987 LHSAA Girls State Championship
Northshore 3 Newman 0 (at Lupin Field, Newman) March 21, 1987

1987-1988 LHSAA Girls State Championship
Northshore 5 Slidell 1 (at Lupin Field, Newman) March 19, 1988

1988-1989 LHSAA Girls State Championship
Northshore 1 Slidell 0 (at Slidell High) February 18, 1989

1989-1990 LHSAA Girls State Championship
Northshore 1 Slidell 0 (at Northshore High) February 17, 1990

1990-1991 LHSAA Girls State Championship
Slidell 3 Mandeville 2 (at Slidell High) February 16, 1991

1991-1992 LHSAA Girls State Championship
Slidell 1 Baton Rouge 0 (at Baton Rouge High) February 22, 1992

1992-1993 LHSAA Girls State Championship
Comeaux defeated Baton Rouge (at Comeaux High) February 20, 1993

1993-1994 LHSAA Girls State Championship
Baton Rouge defeated Lafayette (at Lafayette High) February 19, 1994

1994-1995 LHSAA Girls State Championship
Baton Rouge 2 Ben Franklin 0 (at Baton Rouge High) February 18, 1995

1995-1996 LHSAA Girls State Championships
Div I: Byrd 3 Comeaux 2 (at C.E. Byrd) February 24, 1996
Div II: Sacred Heart 3 Vandebilt 1 OT (at Terrier Field, Vandebilt) February 16, 1996

1996-1997 LHSAA Girls State Championships
Div I: Slidell 3 Woodlawn BR 2 (at Slidell High) March 1, 1997
Div II: Sacred Heart 1 Parkview Baptist 0 (at Jefferson Playground, Jefferson) February 21, 1997

1997-1998 LHSAA Girls State Championships
Div I: Ben Franklin 4 Slidell 2 (at NOSA Fields, UNO) February 27, 1998
Div II: University 4 Loyola 3 (at Loyola) February 24, 1998

1998-1999 LHSAA Girls State Championships
Div I: St. Thomas More 2 Mandeville 2. STM wins 5-4 in PKs (at St. Thomas More) February 26, 1999
Div II: Newman 2 Sacred Heart 0 (at Marconi Meadows, City Park) February 23, 1999

1999-2000 LHSAA Girls State Championship Games
Div I: St. Thomas More 2 Mandeville 0 (at Pan American Stadium) February 26, 2000
Div II: Country Day 1 Sacred Heart 0 (at Marconi Meadows, City Park) February 22, 2000

2000-2001 LHSAA Girls State Championship Games
Div I: Mount Carmel 1 Caddo 0 (OT) (at Tad Gormley Stadium) February 28, 2001
Div II: Newman 2 Parkview Baptist 1 (OT) (at Tad Gormley Stadium) March 1, 2001

2001-2002 LHSAA Girls State Championship Games
Div I: Mount Carmel 2 Mandeville 1 (OT) (at Tad Gormley Stadium) February 23, 2002
Div II: McKinley 2 St. Thomas More 2 McKinley wins 5-4 in PKs (Cougar Stadium, St. Thomas More) February 20, 2002
Div III: Newman 4 Country Day 0 (at Tad Gormley Stadium) February 22, 2002

2002-2003 LHSAA Girls State Championship Games
Div I: Dominican 3 Mandeville 2 (at Tad Gormley) March 8, 2003
Div II: Ben Franklin 4 St. Scholastica 0 (at SSA Sports Complex, St. Scholastica) March 5, 2003
Div III: Sacred Heart 2 Newman 0 (at Tad Gormley) March 7, 2003

2003-2004 LHSAA Girls State Championship Games
Div I: Fontainebleau 4 Mandeville 0 (at Tad Gormley Stadium) February 28, 2004
Div II: Ben Franklin 2 St. Thomas More 1 (OT) (Cougar Stadium, St. Thomas More) February 27, 2004
Div III: Newman 4 Episcopal School of Acadiana 0 (at Tad Gormley Stadium) February 27, 2004

2004-2005 LHSAA Girls State Championship Games
Div I: Mount Carmel 1 Lafayette 1. Mt. Carmel wins 3-1 in PKs. (at Tad Gormley Stadium) February 26, 2005
Div II: Sacred Heart 1 St. Scholastica 0 (at Tad Gormley Stadium) February 26, 2005
Div III: Newman 2 St. Martin's 1 (at Tad Gormley Stadium) February 25, 2005

2005-2006 LHSAA Girls State Championship Games
Div I: Lafayette 1 Barbe 0 (at ULL Soccer Complex) March 4, 2006
Div II: St. Thomas More 3 Vandebilt 1 (at Buddy Marcello Stadium, Vandebilt) March 3, 2006
Div III: Newman 2 Sacred Heart 0 (at ULL Soccer Complex) March 3, 2006

2006-2007 LHSAA Girls State Championship Games
Div I: Dominican 0 Lafayette 0. Dominican 6-5 in PKs. (at Independence Stadium) February 24, 2007
Div II: St. Scholastica 5 Neville 0 (at Neville High) February 23, 2007
Div III: Newman 1 Sacred Heart 0 (at Independence Stadium) February 23, 2007

2007-2008 LHSAA Girls State Championship Games
Div I: St. Thomas More 3 Barbe 0 (at Independence Stadium) February 23, 2008
Div II: Vandebilt 3 St. Michael 0 (Spartan Stadium, Gonzales) February 15, 2008
Division III: St. Louis 2 Sacred Heart 1 (2OT) (at Independence Stadium) February 22, 2008

2008-2009 LHSAA Girls State Championship Games
Division I: St. Scholastica 4 Fontainebleau 0 (at Independence Stadium) February 28, 2009
Division II: Vandebilt 5 Teurlings 0 (at Buddy Marcello Stadium, Vandebilt) February 20, 2009
Div III: St. Louis 4 Sacred Heart 0 (at Independence Stadium) February 27, 2009

2009-2010 LHSAA Girls State Championship Games
Div I: St. Scholastica 1 Mount Carmel 1 (SSA 4-3 in PKs) (at Independence Stadium) February 27, 2010
Div II: St. Louis 2 Vandebilt 0 (at McNeese State) February 27, 2010
Div III: Sacred Heart 1 Catholic New Iberia 0 (4OT) (at Independence Stadium) February 26, 2010

2010-2011 LHSAA Girls State Championship Games
Div I: Dominican 2 St. Scholastica 1 (at Tad Gormley Stadium) February 26, 2011
Div II: Teurlings 2 Vandebilt 1 (at Buddy Marcello Stadium, Vandebilt) February 25, 2011

Div III: Sacred Heart 3 Catholic New Iberia 1 (at Tad Gormley Stadium) February 25, 2011

2011-2012 LHSAA Girls State Championship Games
Div I: Mount Carmel 2 St. Scholastica 1 (at Tad Gormley Stadium) February 25, 2012
Div II: Teurlings 2 Vandebilt 1 (at Tad Gormley Stadium) February 24, 2012
Div III: Sacred Heart 2 Episcopal BR 0 (at Tad Gormley Stadium) February 25, 2012

2012-2013 LHSAA Girls State Championship Games
Div I: Lafayette 2 St. Scholastica 1 (at Tad Gormley Stadium) February 23, 2013
Div II: Ben Franklin 2 Vandebilt 0 (at Tad Gormley Stadium) February 23, 2013
Div III: Sacred Heart 3 Loyola 0 (at Tad Gormley Stadium) February 22, 2013

Head coach records in the Louisiana high school girls' soccer championship games

Tooraj Badie, Newman & Sacred Heart (6-2). Wins: 2001, 2002 (Newman), 2010, 2011, 2012, 2013. Losses: 2008, 2009.
Sean Moser, Sacred Heart (4-4). Wins: 1996, 1997, 2003, 2005. Losses: 1999, 2000, 2006, 2007.
Patrick Summerour, Newman (4-1). Wins: 2004, 2005, 2006, 2007. Loss: 2003.
James Scott, Northshore (4-0). Wins: 1987, 1988, 1989, 1990.
Mike Ortner, St. Scholastica (3-3). Wins: 2007, 2009, 2010. Losses: 2011, 2012, 2013.
Philip Amedee, Vandebilt Catholic (2-4). Wins: 2008, 2009. Losses: 2010, 2011, 2012, 2013.
John Barone, Slidell (2-3). Wins: 1991, 1992. Losses: 1988, 1989, 1990.
Sheila Achee, Baton Rouge (2-2). Wins: 1994, 1995. Losses: 1992, 1993.
Katie Breaux, Lafayette (2-2). Wins: 2006, 2013. Losses: 2005, 2007.
Maggie Millet, Country Day (2-1). Wins: 1980, 1981. Loss: 1983.
Brad Cohen, St. Thomas More (2-1). Wins: 1999, 2000. Loss: 2002.
Sean Esker, Mount Carmel & Mandeville (2-1). Wins: 2001, 2002 (MCA). Loss: 2004 (Mandeville)
Laura Carlin, Ben Franklin (2-0). Wins: 2003, 2004.
John Fell, St. Thomas More (2-0). Wins: 2006, 2008.
Duncan McDonald, St. Louis Catholic (2-0). Wins, 2009, 2010.
Lance Peltier, Teurlings Catholic (2-0). Wins: 2011, 2012.
Travis Smith, Slidell (1-1). Win: 1997. Loss: 1998.
Colin Rocke, Country Day (1-1). Win: 2000. Loss: 2002.
Al Silvas, St. Martin's & Dominican (1-1). Win: 2011 (Dominican). Loss: 2005 (STM).
Pavlos Petrous, Mount Carmel (1-1). Win: 2012. Loss: 2010.
Wayne Grubb, Slidell (1-0). Win: 1985.
Lisa Levermann, Byrd (1-0). Win: 1996.
Mike Rolufs, Ben Franklin (1-0). Win: 1998.
Patti Speaks, University (1-0). Win: 1998.
Bradley Farris, Newman (1-0). Win: 1999.
Ron Bucholtz, McKinley (1-0). Win: 2002.
Jim Barrouquere, Dominican (1-0). Win: 2003.
Rusty Brauner, Fontainebleau (1-0). Win: 2004.
Robert Villio, Mount Carmel (1-0). Win: 2005.
Henrik Madsen, Dominican (1-0). Win: 2007.
Paul Burgess, St. Louis (1-0). Win: 2008.
Jose Ferrand, Ben Franklin (1-0). Win: 2013.

Wendi Frosch Corales, Mandeville (0-3). Losses: 2000, 2002, 2003.
Curtis Stewart, Barbe (0-2). Losses: 2006, 2008.
Chris Hoag, Catholic New Iberia (0-2). Losses: 2010, 2011.
Greg Brozeit, Newman (0-1). Loss: 1987.
Joe Saragusa, Mandeville (0-1). Loss: 1991.
Pat Roche, Ben Franklin (0-1). Loss: 1995.
Ayed Laymoun, Woodlawn BR (0-1). Loss: 1997.
Phil Knowles, Parkview Baptist (0-1). Loss: 1997.
Shelley McMillian, Loyola (0-1). Loss: 1998.
Ken Matthews, Mandeville (0-1). Loss: 1999.
Chase Wooten, Caddo (0-1). Loss: 2001.
Art Lyons, St. Scholastica (0-1). Loss: 2003.
Willie Davis, St. Thomas More (0-1). Loss: 2004.
Terry Morris, St. Scholastica (0-1). Loss: 2005.
Matt Falgout, Vandebilt (0-1). Loss: 2006.
Bret Sanders, Neville (0-1). Loss: 2007.
Anthony Neeson, St. Michael's (0-1). Loss: 2008.
Carly Hotard, Fontainebleau (0-1). Loss: 2009.
Rachel Cohen Schwarz, Teurlings Catholic (0-1). Loss: 2009.
Mark Matlock, Loyola (0-1). Loss: 2013.

High School State MVPs, Gatorade Player of the Year, and the LAprep XI MVP

(boys listed first; girls listed after the semicolon)

YEAR	Div I MVP	Div II MVP	Div III MVP	Gatorade POY	LAprep XI MVP
1982	Tooraj Badie (Shaw); Diane Newman (Newman)				
1983	Elvin Garcia (Warren Easton)				
1984	unknown; unknown				
1985	Jaime Nevarez (Slidell); unknown				
1986	unknown; unknown			Todd Weeldon (Acadiana)	
1987	unknown; unknown			Frank Melia (Bonnabel)	
1988	unknown; Jill Stanley (Northshore)			Matt Werner (Jesuit)	
1989	unknown; unknown			Mike Stephens (Slidell)	
1990	unknown; unknown	unknown		Shane Jeanfreau (De La Salle)	
1991	Jason Kreis (Mandeville); unknown	unknown		Toli Savvaides (De La Salle)	
1992	Kevin Kleinpeter (Catholic BR) and Jason Abney (Slidell); Kathy Krupa (Baton Rouge)	unknown		Toli Savvaides (De La Salle)	
1993	unknown; unknown	unknown		Toli Savvaides (De La Salle)	
1994	unknown; Jenny Streiffer (Baton Rouge)	unknown		Brian Borderlon (De La Salle)	
1995	Josh Burton (Catholic BR); Jenny Streiffer (Baton Rouge)	Dominic Amato (Newman)		David Millet (De La Salle)	
1996	Randy Fortenberry (Mandeville); Jenny Streiffer (Baton Rouge)	Jason Maxwell (Loyola); Nikki Bonilla (Sacred Heart)	Curtis Bush (Newman)	Christian Baldwin (Brother Martin)	
1997	Lane Lombas (Acadiana); Lauren Tatum (Scotlandville)	Stephen Pate (St. Paul's); Jennifer Soileau (Parkview Baptist)	Nik Fusilier (St. Louis)	Stephen Pate (St. Paul's)	
1998	Josh Vidrine (Acadiana); Alyssa Lyon (Ben Franklin)	Paul Watson (St. Paul's); Emily Maxwell (Loyola)	Nik Fusilier (St. Louis)	Scott Aertker (Jesuit); Meggie Tujague (Sacred Heart)	

	Div I MVP	Div II MVP	Div III MVP	GPOY
1999	P.J. Kee (Jesuit); Rachel Cohen (St Thomas More)	Jeremy Laury (Woodlawn); Kelsey Hardy (University) & Casey Godelfer (Newman)	Brad Sutherlin (Newman)	P.J. Kee (Jesuit); Jennifer Talavera (Dominican)
2000	Nick Lambert (Brother Martin); Rachel Cohen (St Thomas More)	Tim Carty and James Pye (St. Paul's); Shellie Harmon (Country Day)	Ryan McCearley (Parkview Baptist)	Ryan McCearley (Parkview Baptist); Rachel Cohen (St Thomas More)
2001	Jason Garey (St. Amant); Kristen Frischertz (Mount Carmel)	Jarrett Garber (St. Thomas More); Kate Ripple (Parkview Baptist)	Dwayne Jones (Newman)	Dwayne Jones (Newman); Shellie Harmon (Country Day)
2002	Michael Touchy (Jesuit); Kristen Frischertz (Mount Carmel) & Susan Marschall (Baton Rouge)	Jonathan Menard (Vandebilt); Ashleigh Gunning (McKinley)	Jonathan Benoit (St. Louis); Katie Couvillion (Newman)	Britton Chauvin (Newman); Shellie Harmon (Country Day)
2003	Casey Steen (Jesuit); Melissa Plannels (Mandeville)	Jonathan Menard (Vandebilt); Rebecca Abbott (Ben Franklin)	Jay Honore (St. Louis); Emily Leefe (Sacred Heart)	Jacobs Marks (Northside); Holly Moran (East Ascension)
2004	Wil Wilson (Central Lafourche); Melissa Garey (St. Amant)	Taylor Pierron (Vandebilt); Rachel Alexander (Parkway)	Joseph Lapira (St. Louis); Meredith Harris (Episcopal BR)	Joseph Lapira (St. Louis); Melissa Garey (St. Amant)
2005	Reece Thomas (Jesuit); Roslyn Jones (Fontainebleau)	Jared Wooley (Vandebilt); Leslie Robichaux (Bishop Sullivan) & Margaret Houser (Sacred Heart)	Marshall Fant (Newman); Mia Scoggin (Newman)	Ned Waller (Newman); Christine Breaux (Dutchtown)
2006	Jarrett Gautreau (Dutchtown); Danielle Jordan (Lafayette)	Gordon Blum (Vandebilt); Kenney Richards (St Thomas More)	Ross Thevenot (St. Louis); Danielle Johnson (Parkview Baptist)	Ross Thevenot (St. Louis); Sarah Benson (Baton Rouge)
2007	Steven Duncan (Jesuit); Hannah Macormic (Mandeville)	Adam Saloom (St. Thomas More); Kelly Gautreaux (St Scholastica)	Michael Lapira (St. Louis); Paige Pointer (Newman)	Andrew Mullins (Jesuit); Hannah Macormic (Mandeville)
2008	Nick Flowers (Caddo); Kellie Murphy (St Thomas More)	Jordan Miller (Teurlings); Jordan Picou (Vandebilt)	Michael Lapira (St. Louis); Melissa Minton (St. Louis)	Nick Flowers (Caddo); Kellie Murphy (St Thomas More)
2009	Brennan Randel (Captain Shreve); Tricia Johnson (St Scholastica)	Michael Hollier (Teurlings); Cayla Chatman (Vandebilt)	Matt Savoie (Newman); Natalie Ieyoub (St. Louis)	Patrick Mullins (Jesuit); Tricia Johnson (St Scholastica)
2010	Steven Cabos (Jesuit); Danielle Beatty (St Scholastica)	Michael Hollier (Teurlings); Rasheema Clark (St. Louis)	Mason Neveu (Newman); Katherine Moody (Sacred Heart)	Steven Cabos (Jesuit); Emily Cancienne (Baton Rouge)

	Div I MVP	Div II MVP	D III MVP	GPOY	LAprep MVP
2011	Adrian McInnis (St. Paul's); Katherine Cuntz (Dominican)	Louie Jones (St. Louis); Sarah Hollier (Teurlings)	Mallery Mele (Northlake); Katherine Moody (Sacred Heart)	Adrian McInnis (St. Paul's); Katherine Cuntz (Dominican)	
2012	Phillip Hicks (Jesuit); Elizabeth Manuel (Mandeville)	Chris Cironi (St. Louis); Meghan Philp (Vandebilt)	Gary Lawrence (Country Day); Keely Davis (Episcopal BR)	Phillip Hicks (Jesuit); Delaney Sheehan (Mandeville)	Phillip Hicks (Jesuit)
2013	Ethan Judice (Lafayette); Delaney Sheehan (Mandeville)	Brock Hollier (Beau Chene); Hannah Savoie (Teurlings)	Adam Clausen (Episcopal BR); Sarah Martin (Sacred Heart)	Ethan Judice (Lafayette); Delaney Sheehan (Mandeville)	Brock Hollier (Beau Chene)

St. Paul's Holiday Invitational Championship Game results:

St. Paul's Holiday Invitational is widely regarded as the top high school soccer tournament in Louisiana. There is good reason why. The results, compared to the playoff results, are quite similar. In the 20 years since the 1992 St. Paul's Tournament, 17 of the 40 St. Paul's Tournament finalists won a state championship. 5 more were state runner-up. For the last seven seasons, one of the Finalists at St. Paul's has won state.

1984: unknown
1985: unknown
1986: unknown
1987: Catholic BR 4 Rummel 3 (PKs)
1988: Catholic BR beat Northshore
1989: unknown
1990: unknown
1991: Catholic BR 3 De La Salle 0
1992: Catholic BR 2 De La Salle 1
1993: Bishop Sullivan
1994: Catholic BR 2 Jesuit 0
1995: Mandeville 3 St. Paul's 0
1996: St. Paul's 4 Baton Rouge 3
1997: Northshore 1 St. Paul's 0 (5-4 PKs)
1998: Jesuit 4 Vandebilt 1
1999: Jesuit 2 Northshore 0
2000: Jesuit 2 Caddo 0
2001: Vandebilt 3 Jesuit 1
2002: Ben Franklin 1 Vandebilt 0
2003: Vandebilt 4 Catholic BR 1 (played at Vandebilt due to weather)
2004: St. Paul's 1 Vandebilt 0
2005: Jesuit 5 St. Paul's 2
2006: Jesuit 5 Caddo 0
2007: Caddo 2 Brother Martin 1 (10-9 PKs)
2008: Jesuit 4 Caddo 0
2009: Jesuit 3 St. Paul's 1
2010: Jesuit 1 St. Paul's 0
2011: Jesuit 3 Brother Martin 0
2012: Jesuit 3 Catholic BR 2

Louisiana Referees and Assessors of Note

Louisiana has produced some of America's best referees and assessors.

Nationals-level referees:

Andrew Barnes (also appointed to FIFA list)
Stephen Binning
Kyle Borne
Mark deClout
Douglas Dutt
Mitch Jacobs
Harlan Matthews
Tyler Mitcham
Caesar Munoz
Jennifer Politz
Michelle Tubre
Mike Williams

National assessors:

Stephen Binning
Harlan Matthews
Bob Sanders
Bob Wertz

For those wishing to contact me about this book, I can be reached at LSUsoccerbum@hotmail.com.

Made in the USA
Columbia, SC
11 May 2025